Creative Ideas for Pastoral Liturgy

MARRIAGE SERVICES, WEDDING BLESSINGS and ANNIVERSARY THANKSGIVINGS

Creative Ideas
for Pastoral Liturgy

Marriage Services,
Wedding Blessings and
Anniversary Thanksgivings

Jan Brind and Tessa Wilkinson

CANTERBURY
PRESS
Norwich

First published in 2009 by the Canterbury Press Norwich
(a publishing imprint of Hymns Ancient & Modern Limited,
a registered charity)
13–17 Long Lane, London EC1A 9PN

www.scm-canterburypress.co.uk

British Library Cataloguing in Publication data

A catalogue record for this book is available
from the British Library

ISBN 978-1-85311-928-6

Typeset by Regent Typesetting, London
Printed in the UK by the
MPG Books Group

This book is dedicated with love to our parents

Janet and 'Kempie' Kemp
June and Jack Osbourn

CONTENTS

INTRODUCTION

In today's society, although many couples decide to live together permanently, fewer are committing to a legally binding marriage. So when a couple do decide to 'tie the knot' and to do so within a church service in the sight of God, with their family and friends present, it is always a time for real celebration, and a chance for the church to do what a church should do best – reach out in love and welcome.

However, it is worth reflecting that, because weddings can now take place in so many other venues, people do not always think first of their local church. And yet, as well as often being a beautiful building, a church can provide so many of the things considered part and parcel of a wedding – the minister, who also acts as the registrar, the flowers, an organist and choir, and bells. And all this comes with a timeless, prayerful and holy sense of God's presence. It seems that churches have something to learn from other public venues which advertise themselves for weddings. One way of getting around this might be for a church to produce a wedding information leaflet, describing what it offers and giving details of local caterers, dressmakers, photographers, wine merchants, car hire firms, travel agents and so on. A regular advertisement in the parish magazine or local paper is a good way to remind people of their local church. And don't forget the church website! Stage a weddings exhibition in the church. The church can be filled for a whole weekend with wedding dresses, flowers, photographs of past weddings and so on, and people can be encouraged to come and look. Parishioners might be on hand to talk about what is possible and what resources the church can provide. As well as the church, these resources might include the parish room for the reception and caterers from the congregation. This is when a leaflet, also giving costs, might be useful for couples to take away. The leaflet might also give a short description of the church's marriage preparation course and information about the reading of the Banns. If we believe that the best wedding is a Christian one, then we need to be proud of what we offer and shout about it from the roof tops!

Being supportive, encouraging and welcoming from the moment the couple contact the minister or parish secretary to talk over a possible wedding is very important. This support, encouragement and welcome should continue in the weeks leading up to the marriage service, as the couple are helped with the arrangements for the day when they are to make their vows to God and to each other, and afterwards as they begin to walk the road together as a married couple.

The stories and circumstances of each couple who decide to marry are always unique. In this book we have tried to address some of the different scenarios and situations that may occur and we give some ideas and resources that may help the couple, together with the minister, plan a wedding that will feel special and be a reflection of their lives. We have worked around the given authorized liturgy for marriage, adding a rich tapestry of readings, songs, hymns, prayers and music.

Of course there are very many suitable readings, songs and hymns that might be used – our choices can only be suggestions. Readings in particular are readily available to view on the internet using one of the many search engines. Searching by title, or even a single sentence, along with the writer's name, will result in a number of websites that contain the text. If you wish to reproduce a reading in a service sheet, please remember that the laws of copyright apply and that you may need to obtain permission from the publisher. The Society of Authors provides a guide to permissions on its website: www.societyofauthors.org/publications/quick_guide_permissions. And most people have favourite songs, hymns or pieces of music which are meaningful to them and which they would like sung or played at their wedding. We have deliberately suggested songs and hymns that are perhaps more unusual than those often chosen and they may be found in more than one hymn book. Copyright permission for most hymns and songs is covered either by the Christian Copyright Licence (www.ccli.co.uk) or by Calamus (www.decanimusic.co.uk). Very often the music director and/or organist at the church where the wedding is to take place will spend time with the couple in advance, listening to their requests, playing pieces of music, and helping them decide what might work well. Is the choir needed? Might there be an anthem? If not, can recorded music be played through a sound system during the signing of the register?

We have not made specific suggestions for flowers or church decoration – but remember that this, too, along with making the church look fresh and clean, is a chance for the church to celebrate with the couple as members of the congregation spend time making everything look beautiful for the special day.

For many people, being in a church for a service is something unusual and the words and symbolism may feel strange and unfamiliar. We hope that our words and suggestions will feel comfortable for everyone. The welcome at the beginning of a service is so important and allows the minister to tell people a little of what is to happen. Encourage everyone to join in responses enthusiastically! This, too, will put the couple getting married at ease.

As well as ideas for different wedding scenarios we include in this book some ideas for the reading of Banns, and for the congregation to welcome a couple back to church after a honeymoon. We have also given a short liturgy for the ending of a marriage. We feel that the church community should be able to give support and loving pastoral care at this most painful and difficult time, particularly if the people concerned are members of the congregation.

We are very grateful to Revd Richard Deimel and Ann Lewin for their encouragement and help. Richard Deimel has given us words and ideas for rites to use within marriage services that include welcoming children and families, and remembering a spouse who has died. Ann Lewin is a writer and author of *Words by the Way: Ideas and Resources for Use Throughout the Christian Year*. She has graciously allowed us to print in full her 'Suggestion for an introduction to a marriage service after a divorce'.

We would also like to thank David Davies, Diocesan Music Adviser, Sub-organist and Director of the girl choristers at Guildford Cathedral. David has arranged the music for *I will be beside you*.

The Bible readings that we have quoted come from the New Revised Standard Version.

The aim of this resource book is to make life as easy as possible for the person planning a service, so a CD containing all the material in the book is included with it. We hope the CD will enable the user to download the service, remove anything they do not want, add their own words, or choose some from other parts of the book which they can cut and paste, and so make the service their own. Once the service is personalized all they have to do is print it off. Also on the CD are the illustrations. These are included so that they, too, can be downloaded and personalized.

Jan Brind and
Tessa Wilkinson

PART ONE: PREPARATION

CREATING A USEFUL FOLDER

If a couple decide to get married in church this presents a wonderful opportunity. The minister and, with careful thought, the people can become fully involved in the planning and celebration of the great day. The couple may or may not be known to the congregation, but this is always a time to reach out in love and welcome. Giving the couple resources to look at in advance – service sheets, ideas for readings, songs, hymns, music CDs, local catering and photography possibilities and so on – might be very helpful. As with baptisms, and funerals and thanksgivings, the minister will have married many couples, but this couple will almost certainly be getting married for the first time! So here are some ideas to gather together and put in a 'Useful Folder'.

The 'Useful Folder'

Remember that this is a 'living' folder, which will be added to and revised. Put several copies of each item into plastic pockets so that the couple can take one out and keep it to look at.

Readings

We have chosen some of the better known and used Bible readings in the following service scenarios, but there are many others. There must be one reading from the Bible, but there can be other readings as well. We have found some slightly unusual ones by looking at websites. A huge selection of readings can by found by typing 'Readings for Weddings' into the search engine on a computer. And there are poems and reflections, too, or short texts from favourite books. Put a selection in the folder – this is really useful for people who are not sure what they want.

Hymns, songs and music

Place a list of suitable songs and hymns in the folder. The couple will probably know which favourite hymns they would like, usually ones they grew up with and which they know their friends will know and be able to sing. But there are others, particularly songs by contemporary composers, that have been written specifically for weddings. It is well worth discovering them. We have made a list in this book. When it comes to recorded music we give suggestions – again the couple may well have their own ideas, and our suggestions are from our own CD collection. And we list some CDs in the Useful CDs section. Recorded music will really only be needed if there is no choir, or if the organist does not want to play during the signing of the register. You might like to invest in one or two CDs to keep in the folder.

IDEAS TO MAKE THE SPECIAL DAY EVEN MORE SPECIAL

Here are some ideas to add something extra to the day. Some of these ideas might be placed in the 'Useful Folder' for prospective couples to see, along with your own ideas. See also the ideas we have suggested in some of the services.

- Make an altar frontal, banners and a stole – make these personal to the couple and choose colours that will go with their chosen flowers. (See 'How to Make a Paper Altar Frontal' on page 117, 'How to Make and Hang Banners' on page 113 and 'How to Make a Stole' on page 121.)
- Ask the couple for a photo and place this on the church notice board with their names and the date of the wedding. On the day place a notice outside the church giving these details.
- If guests have a long way to travel, and might arrive a little early, make sure they are welcomed. A cup of tea and the availability of a cloakroom might be much needed.
- Consider offering a catering service. Members of the congregation may enjoy preparing and serving food for the reception. They might wear matching aprons to give a co-ordinated look. (See 'How to Make an Apron' on page 139 and 'How to Put a Design on to Fabric Using Appliqué' on page 128.)
- Ask guests to bring a 'memory' to the wedding – this might be a photo or a written story. These can be gathered on the day and put in an album afterwards for the couple to keep.
- Make up a display board of photos of the couple going back over the years up to the present. Have it on view in the church and then take it to the reception.
- It is always good to have a record of guests who come to the wedding. A book by the church door is one way of doing this – choose an attractive book and

provide a good pen. Or place cards on the pews or chairs that people can fill in. (See design templates of pew card designs on pages 141–44.)

- Provide special bags for the children present – spray-paint the names of the couple getting married and the date. Put small 'quiet' toys and books inside – tiny Bible story books are a good idea. (See 'How to Make a Drawstring Bag for Children' on page 138.)
- Give party-poppers to everyone as they arrive in the church. When the couple are pronounced 'man and wife' the poppers can be let off in celebration.
- Make 'Bags for Life'. (See sections 'Reading of Banns in Church Before a Marriage Service' on page 9 and 'Welcome Back to Church After a Honeymoon' on page 97.) (See 'How to Make a "Bag for Life"' on page 136.)
- Give everyone in the church a candle – these can be lit from the Paschal Candle during the service. This symbolizes a shared journey with the couple getting married.
- Give cards and pens to everyone so that they can write their own wishes and prayers for the couple – these can be brought to the altar during the service. (See blessing card template on page 144.)
- Write the couple's names around the edge of nightlights. Give one to each person at the end of the service to take home and light for the couple. Or, with slightly larger candles, write the names and a short blessing. (See 'How to Put a Design on to a Candle' on page 131.)
- Give everyone a card to take home with a blessing giving the couple's names and the date and place of the wedding. (See templates of cards to take home on page 146.)
- Make heart-shaped biscuits or chocolate fudge, wrapped in cellophane and ribbon, to give to everyone at the end of the service – the children might hand them around in a basket. (See 'How to Make Heart-Shaped Biscuits' on page 147 and 'How to Make Simple Chocolate Fudge' on page 148.)
- Provide cake for the congregation, choir, organist, flower arrangers and cleaners etc., and arrange for it to be given out at the first service after the wedding to say thank you – or do this on return from honeymoon.
- Give a special card to the couple to welcome them back from honeymoon – this might have the time, date and church name and photo of the church on one side, and information about services and church activities on the other side.
- Welcome the couple back to church from their honeymoon with coffee and cake.
- Send anniversary cards to the couple from the church congregation. (See templates for anniversary cards on page 145.)

PROCESSIONS

When planning a church service it is important to think about how to 'process' in and out of the church at the beginning and end of the service. Traditionally, at the start of a service, the groom is up at the front of the nave with the best man, and the bride enters by the west door and walks down the aisle with her father and is 'given away' to the safekeeping of the groom. For many couples this is still what they want to do. But for some this does not feel right, so it is important to plan the entrance to suit each couple's circumstances. For instance, if the couple have been living together and already have children, it might seem inappropriate for the father of the bride to 'give his daughter away', when clearly this happened some while ago. In this situation the couple, bride and groom, might walk down the aisle together with their children at the beginning of the service.

Here are some possibilities:

- The bride enters with her father and joins the groom waiting at the front.
- The bride enters with her mother and joins the waiting groom.
- The bride walks down the aisle with her father followed by the groom walking down with his mother.
- The bride is led down the aisle by her father and mother.
- The couple enter together.
- The couple enter together with the best man and/or chief bridesmaid as their 'supporters' and the bridesmaids and pageboys.
- The bride walks down the aisle with a significant person other than her father or mother.
- The couple enter leading the procession, with their extended families following behind.
- The couple enter in a procession, being led down the aisle by their children and families.
- The couple are together at the front of the church, waiting for everyone to arrive.

- The couple walk down the aisle with their child/children carrying their wedding rings on a cushion.

Leaving the church at the end of the service is a little more straightforward. The newly married couple lead the procession down the aisle to the west door, followed by bridesmaids and pageboys, parents – bride's mother with groom's father, bride's father with groom's mother – close family, guests and friends.

READING OF BANNS IN CHURCH BEFORE A MARRIAGE SERVICE

The calling of the Banns in church before a wedding can often pass by with little attention, added on to the notices at the beginning, middle or end of the service. The law requires the Banns to be read on three Sundays. The couple may, or may not, be present but, as the Banns need not be read on consecutive Sundays, the couple have an opportunity to plan to be there. The reading of Banns is the first legal step the couple are taking together as they approach their marriage and, although the Banns are often read without supporting prayer, there are two very beautiful prayers given in the *Common Worship* Supplementary Texts that can be read to make the moment a little more special. The couple might be invited to come to the front of the church so this becomes a time of welcome and support and anticipation. They might have the engagement ring blessed. They can also be given a 'Bag for Life'. This can be presented to the couple on the first or the last Sunday that the Banns are read as a gift from the congregation to sustain and encourage them during the time leading up to the marriage.

Prayer of Commitment

Ask a member of the congregation to come forward to speak these words, or others, before the bag is presented

> N and N, we will continue to hold you in our prayers
> as you prepare for your wedding day.
> We will support and encourage you in the coming weeks as you
> prepare to make your promises and commit your lives to God
> and to each other.

We offer you this Bag for Life that you may find in it a source of comfort in times of need or stress.
It comes with love from the people of God in this place.
May God bless you and fill you with peace.
May God bless you and fill you with peace.

Action

Make a 'Bag for Life' (see 'How to Make a "Bag for Life"' on page 136) and fill it with special things to support the couple in the weeks between the reading of the Banns and the wedding. This is often a very stressful time, with so much to organize and so many people's feelings and needs to consider and include. The bag can have a large label on it to explain what is inside, or the contents can be placed in the bag at the time of reading the Banns, in front of everyone, so the congregation knows what is inside and why it has been chosen. Here are some ideas (see label templates on page 137):

- **A candle** - to light the way
- **A Prayer Card** - a reminder that God is ever present
- **Bath bubbles** - to relax in
- **Aromatherapy oil** - to soothe frayed nerves
- **A comedy DVD** - to share laughter
- **Fizzy water** - to refresh and revitalise
- **Chocolate** - to break and share
- **Wine** - to break open in case of emergency

KEEPING THE COST DOWN FINANCIALLY AND ETHICALLY

Weddings can be enormously expensive. However, there are many ways to keep the cost down while still making the day really special and memorable. The most important thing is that two people want to marry each other and spend the rest of their lives together, and that they want to ask God to bless that commitment in the sacrament of marriage. They want to make this commitment to God, in church, and in front of their families and friends. Their families and friends can help them plan and execute a day that will not cost the earth. And, indeed, the wedding will not literally 'cost the earth' if people want to think 'ethical' and 'green'. Below are some ideas that might save a bit of money, followed by ways in which a wedding might be 'ethical and green'.

Keeping the financial cost down

Wedding planner

Ask a special friend to help you plan the wedding.

Wedding invitations

Design your own invitations on a computer. Buy paper or card and envelopes from a discount stationery store.

Wedding dress

Make your own or look in smart second-hand clothes shops, or look on eBay.

Bridesmaids' dresses

Make your own or look on eBay.

Transport

Polish the family car and decorate it with ribbons to make it look festive. Be imaginative about transport. See what is available from family and friends.

Flowers

Ask people in advance to provide flowers from their gardens. Guide them with colour ideas. If you are organized enough you can ask people to plant flower seeds in advance to go with the colour scheme. The bride and bridesmaids can carry loosely tied bunches of garden flowers. In winter months use greenery and berries tied up with ribbons the same colour as the bridesmaids' dresses. Ask the church flower team for their ideas. The flowers can be taken from the church to the reception. Or put ribbons at the end of pews instead of flowers. Both flowers and ribbons can be bought from wholesale flower markets at greatly reduced prices if someone is prepared to go very early in the morning.

Candles

Buy multi-packs of cheap and chunky candles – either white, ivory or in colours to match the flowers and dresses. You might attach a single flower, or a small sprig, or a piece of ribbon to match the colour scheme, to each candle (see 'Decorating Candles with Ribbon and Flowers' on page 134). The candles can be taken on to the reception and placed on the tables.

Service sheets

Design your own service sheets on a computer. Thread ribbons to match the colour scheme through the sheets to make them look special.

Music

Do you have any friends who could form a small music group to lead the singing at the service, or a friend who plays the piano or sings, and who could then provide gentle background music at the reception?

The rings

Rings vary enormously in price and can be bought second-hand as well as new.

Confetti

Make your own out of tissue paper using a hole punch, or scatter handfuls of rose or larkspur petals from baskets, or use rice.

The reception

Have the reception in the church hall, the parish room, a local school, an upstairs room in a pub, or in someone's garden with a few gazebos in case of rain. A hired marquee tends to be a very expensive option unless you can hire one from a local scout or guide group.

Decorations at the reception

Place tablecloths over long tables and arrange groups of chunky candles and glass tumblers of flowers at intervals. Helium-filled balloons are very effective. Anchor them in twos and threes to the centres of the tables. Choose colours to fit the theme.

The feast

Ask people to 'bring and share' plates of food. It is safer if you plan a menu in advance and ask specific people to bring specific items.

The drink

Although it is traditional to have champagne at weddings, anything fizzy will do. Make a fruit punch and put it in a large glass bowl. Add pieces of fruit and heart-shaped ice cubes.

The cake

Ask a friend to bake the cake – either traditional fruit cake, or chocolate gateau, or carrot cake. A pyramid made with meringues or profiteroles looks very impressive – several people might help with this.

Photography and video film

Ask several friends with digital cameras to be the official photographers.

Being ethical and green

Wedding invitations

Design your own invitations on a computer and use recycled paper or card. Use envelopes made from recycled paper.

Wedding clothes

The wedding dress, bridesmaids' and pageboys' clothes, and groom's clothes, can be made from Fair Trade and/or organic cotton.

Flowers

See above. If buying flowers choose Fair Trade varieties.

Candles

Ask your nearest L'Arche Community to make candles. You can give them a special order so that you have exactly what you want. Look L'Arche up on the internet to find your nearest community.

Transport

Ask guests to share transport. Give people details of buses and trains with their invitations and arrange for a coach or minibus to collect from stations.

Service sheets

Design your own service sheets on a computer. Print them off on recycled paper. Thread ribbons through the sheets to make them look special.

Cards from Christian Aid

Christian Aid has produced cards to give away to guests at weddings. The cards are aimed at people who profess to be Christian but who are not regular church-goers. On one side of each card is a photograph from the developing world and an explanation of what Christians believe about marriage, together with a greeting and a space for a personalized message. On the other side is information about Christian Aid's work with the world's poorest communities. The cards can be bought in packs of six by telephoning 08700 787788 or by visiting your local Christian bookshop.

Confetti

See above.

The reception

In summertime have the reception in a garden – have a few gazebos in case of rain.

The feast

As far as is possible use fairly traded food.

The drink

Buy Fair Trade wine. Make a fruit punch using delicious Fair Trade fruit juice. The Co-op or Traidcraft has a good range. Serve Fair Trade tea, coffee and sugar.

The cake

Bake a cake using Fair Trade ingredients. Buy and decorate a Fair Trade fruit cake.

Gifts

Ask for ethical gifts – either gifts from Fair Trade or charity catalogues (e.g. Oxfam, Christian Aid, Traidcraft, Cafod, Tear Fund, Habitat for Humanity, etc.) or gifts, given or bought in your name, that go to the charity (e.g. Send a Cow, Oxfam, Christian Aid). Gifts can be ordered from websites, so put their web addresses on the invitations.

A GLOSSARY OF CHURCHSPEAK

Sometimes the words we use in our church services need explaining to people who are not used to 'churchspeak'. We hope this glossary of some of the words used will be helpful to those people who are planning a church service and who may find the words unfamiliar.

Affirmation of faith	Statement of belief – in this case what Christians believe
Absolution	Forgiveness, pardon
Acclamation	Praise
Betrothal	Binding with a promise, engagement
Blessing of the people	Blessing given by the priest at the end of a service to ask God to watch over those present
Canticle	Psalm
Celebration	A service that is full of thanks and praise
Cohabitation	Two people living together
Commitment	Pledge or promise
Common Worship	Name given to the revision of Church of England services in 2000
Creed	Faith, statement of belief – in this case what Christians believe
Dismissal	Sending out at the end of a service
Entrusting	Handing over to the care of God
Epistle	Letter in the New Testament written by a follower of Jesus

Eternal	Everlasting, unending, ceaseless, timeless, undying
Eternal presence	God with us at all times
Eternity	Time without end, perpetuity, infinity
Eucharist	Thanksgiving, as in a service of Holy Communion
Gospel	Good news, readings from Matthew, Mark, Luke or John in the New Testament
Grace	Blessing, kindness, gift from God
Hallowed	Holy
Holy Communion	Eucharist, a service where bread and wine (Christ's body and blood) are consecrated and shared in his memory
Intercession	Prayer to God on behalf of the people
Lectern	Raised desk where the Bible may be read
Litany	Set of prayers with common response by the congregation
Liturgy	Public worship – including words and use of space
Mercy	Compassion, forgiveness, kindness, healing, pity
Ministering	Giving of oneself for others
Nuptial	Marriage, wedding
Offertory, Offering	Offering of bread and wine during a Eucharist, collection of money during a service
Paschal Candle	Large candle lit on Easter Eve as a sign that Christ is risen. It continues to be lit during Eastertide and at baptisms, weddings and funerals
Penitence	Repentance, atonement, remorse, sorrow
Preface	Introduction
Prevail	Triumph, win through, succeed, overcome
Pulpit	Raised place in a church from which sermons are delivered
Put asunder	Take apart, separate
Reconciliation	Making peace with, settlement, understanding, bringing together
Redeemer	Jesus, saviour, liberator, rescuer, one who mends
Reflections	Memories, thoughts, related words after a reading

Renew the face of the earth	Restore and make new again God's creation in terms of peace and justice
Resurrection	Rebirth, reappearance, restoration, life after death
Righteous	Good, moral, just, blameless, honourable, honest
Sacrament	The bread and wine at Holy Communion – a visible sign of Christ's body and blood
Salvation	Deliverance, rescue, recovery, escape, release
Saviour	Jesus, redeemer, rescuer, liberator
Sermon	Address, talk, oration, tribute
Solemnization of a Union	Making a marriage official
Stole	Scarf worn by a priest or deacon, a vestment
Testimony	Statement of faith, proof, evidence, witness
The Collect	A prayer themed for the day which 'collects' all the other prayers together
The Dismissal	The blessing and 'sending out' at the end of a service
The Gathering	The beginning of worship when the assembly or congregation are 'gathered together' for worship
The Lord's Prayer	The prayer Jesus taught us which begins 'Our Father …'
The Peace	A time to greet each other and share Christ's peace – particularly before Holy Communion
Transformed	Changed
Trespasses	Sins, wrongdoings, infringements, encroachments
Troth	Promise
Union	Joining, coming together
Verily	Truthfully, beyond doubt, really, rightly
Vestments	Clothes worn by a priest or deacon for a ceremony
Victory	Triumph, win, success

PART TWO: MARRIAGE SERVICES

ORDER FOR A MARRIAGE SERVICE

Introduction

The Welcome
Preface
The Declarations
The Collect
Readings
Sermon

The Marriage

The Vows
The Giving of Rings
The Proclamation
The Blessing of the Marriage
Registration of the Marriage
Prayers
The Dismissal

MARRIAGE SERVICE

Basic service

Here are some resources for a marriage which, in the main, follows the traditional pattern. We have inserted an opportunity for a symbolic meeting and greeting of the families of the bride and groom. By including this in the marriage ceremony it gives special significance to the fact that the two families are now linked and, in one sense joined, by the marriage of the bride and groom. Neither family has 'lost' a family member; rather they have both gained a new one.

Bible Readings

How good it is when families live together in unity

How very good and pleasant it is
when kindred live together in unity!
It is like the precious oil on the head,
running down upon the beard,
on the beard of Aaron,
running down over the collar of his robes.
It is like the dew of Hermon,
which falls on the mountains of Zion.
For there the LORD ordained his blessing,
life for evermore.

Psalm 133

Abide in my love that your joy may be complete

As the Father has loved me, so I have loved you; abide in my love. If you keep my commandments, you will abide in my love, just as I have kept my Father's commandments and abide in his love. I have said these things to you so that my joy may be in you, and that your joy may be complete.

John 15.9–11

Being rooted and grounded in love

For this reason I bow my knees before the Father, from whom every family in heaven and on earth takes its name. I pray that, according to the riches of his glory, he may grant that you may be strengthened in your inner being with power through his Spirit, and that Christ may dwell in your hearts through faith, as you are being rooted and grounded in love. I pray that you may have the power to comprehend, with all the saints, what is the breadth and length and height and depth, and to know the love of Christ that surpasses knowledge, so that you may be filled with all the fullness of God.

Now to him who by the power at work within us is able to accomplish abundantly far more than all we can ask or imagine, to him be glory in the church and in Christ Jesus to all generations, for ever and ever.

Ephesians 3.14–21

Other Readings

I love you this much
Author unknown

I love you this much.
Enough to do anything for you, give my life, my love,
my heart and my soul to you and for you.
Enough to willingly give all of my time, efforts, thoughts, talents, trust and prayers to you.
Enough to want to protect you, care for you, guide you, hold you, comfort you, listen to you, and cry to you and with you.
Enough to be completely comfortable with you, act silly around you,
never have to hide anything from you, and be myself with you.
I love you enough to share all of my sentiments, dreams, goals, fears, hopes, and worries, my entire life with you.
Enough to want the best for you, to wish for your successes, and to hope for the fulfilment of all your endeavours.
Enough to keep my promises to you
and pledge my loyalty and faithfulness to you.
Enough to cherish your friendship, adore your personality, respect your values and see you for who you are.

I love you enough to fight for you,
compromise for you, and sacrifice myself for you if need be.
Enough to miss you incredibly when
we're apart, no matter what length.
Enough to believe in our relationship, to stand by it through
the worst of times,
to have faith in our strength as a couple, and to never give up
on us.
Enough to spend the rest of my life with you,
be there for you when you need or want me,
and never, ever want to leave you or live without you.
I love you this much.

On marriage
Kahlil Gibran
From *The Prophet*

Then Almitra spoke again and said, And what of Marriage,
master?
And he answered saying:
You were born together, and together you shall be for
evermore.
You shall be together when the white wings of death scatter
your days.
Aye, you shall be together even in the silent memory of God.
But let there be spaces in your togetherness.
And let the winds of the heavens dance between you.
Love one another, but make not a bond of love:
Let it rather be a moving sea between the shores of your souls.
Fill each other's cup but drink not from one cup.
Give one another of your bread but eat not from the same loaf.
Sing and dance together and be joyous, but let each one of you
be alone,
Even as the strings of a lute are alone though they quiver with
the same music.
Give your hearts, but not into each other's keeping.
For only the hand of Life can contain your hearts.
And stand together yet not too near together:
For the pillars of the temple stand apart,
And the oak tree and cypress grow not in each other's shadow.

The Rite of the Meeting of Families

Parents (and/or step-parents) and siblings of the couple are invited to come and join the couple. All hold hands in a circle as the minister prays

> In the Bible we hear that God's plan is for children to leave their parents and begin a new family through marriage. But we are also told that we should always honour and love our parents, who have given us so much. So we pray that N and N will share a deep love with their parents, in the new context of their marriage. We pray, too, that deep links of sharing will grow between the two families who are now joined through the marriage of N and N.
> **Amen**

All in the circle may exchange hugs and kisses before the parents and siblings return to their seats

Prayers

For the gift of life and love,
for N and N as they begin their journey together,
for families and friends,
we pray to the Lord.
Lord, hold us in your love.

For the gift of children,
for bread broken and shared,
for the joy of growing old together,
we pray to the Lord.
Lord, hold us in your love.

In times of struggle and difficulty,
in times of pain and hurt,
in times of questioning and challenge,
we pray to the Lord.
Lord, hold us in your love.

When we need to forgive,
when we need forgiveness,
when we need healing,
we pray to the Lord.
Lord, hold us in your love.

For today and tomorrow,
for what the future may hold,
for your Holy Spirit moving in our lives,
we pray to the Lord.
Lord, hold us in your love.

**The Blessing
and Dismissal**

Now go in peace from this place,
to live your lives held in God's love
and surrounded by God's truth,
and the blessing of God almighty,
the Father, the Son and the Holy Spirit
be with you and remain with you always.
Amen

**Suggested Hymns
and Songs**

As two we love are wed
(*Common Ground*)

At this marriage celebration
(This book, p. 29)

I will be beside you
(This book, p. 30)

Love changes everything
(Sheet music from The Really Useful Company)

May you walk with Christ beside you
(*Be Still and Know*)

O, heaven is in my heart
(*Songs of Fellowship*)

Suggested Music

Love changes everything
CD: *Aspects of Love*, Andrew Lloyd Webber, Polydor Group

Psallite Deo (This is the day)
CD: *Joy in the Morning*, Taizé Community, Ateliers et Presses de Taizé

The Lord bless you and keep you
CD: *Gloria: The Sacred Music of John Rutter*, John Rutter
Collegium Records

Song

At this marriage celebration

1 At this marriage celebration
   Friends and loved ones gather near;
   Witness to a vowed intention
   By these two whom we hold dear.

2 Rings, as symbols of this wedding,
   Shall be given with a kiss;
   Love and wonder, joy and blessing,
   Heaven sent for earthly bliss.

3 In their marriage we will keep them
   As companions on the way;
   Walk with them through rain and sunshine,
   Give support 'til end of day.

4 Lord, we pray that you will hold them
   In your Spirit's warm embrace;
   And in all the years surround them
   With your precious gift of grace.

5 As their lives near journey's ending
   May their love stay firm and true;
   Hearts entwined, for ever cherished,
   Sanctified and blessed anew.

Text © Jan Brind, 2004
This song can be sung to Love Divine, or Laus Deo (Redhead No. 46), or any tune with an 87 87 metre

Song

I will be beside you

1 I will be beside you through the years
   In your joyful laughter and your silent tears
   Should you fail to see me, do not be dismayed
   I will be beside you all the way.

2 When your hearts are singing I am found
   Where your feet are dancing this is holy ground
   Loving one another, living every day
   I am there beside you all the way.

3 If you're in a shadow I'll be there
   When you're feeling lonely and your souls despair
   Comfort one another, do not be afraid
   I am still beside you all the way.

4 In the thoughts you're thinking I am heard
   In the meals you share and in the spoken word
   Breaking bread together, at the end of day
   I am there beside you all the way.

5 And at journey's ending I'll be there
   Take my hand and feel my warm and gentle care
   I will lead you onwards, trust me when I say
   We will be together all the way.

Jan Brind

I will be beside you

Jan Brind Arr. David Davies

MARRIAGE SERVICE AFTER A COUPLE HAVE LIVED TOGETHER

The following resources are appropriate for a couple getting married who have already lived together for some time. Here are words which acknowledge what has gone before and which celebrate a new beginning. There is also an opportunity for family and friends to write their own wishes and blessings for the couple.

The Welcome   N and N, you have been living and sharing your lives together for the last *xx*. Today you have come to make your marriage vows before God, in the presence of your family and your friends.
We thank God for the life you have already shared. We pray that the Holy Spirit will guide you in the years to come. May these years be full of love and adventure, in Jesus' name.
Amen

The Preface   The gift of love has come to N and N.
Love is the true meaning of life. No money can buy it.
It is a gift from God, who is love.
True love needs people to be faithful to each other for ever.
This is hard, but God's Holy Spirit can make it work.
So N and N have come to church to make their vows in God's house, and to ask for God's help in keeping them.
Let us pray with them now that they will be blessed as they make their vows, and that they will keep them for ever.
Let us all pray in silence for a while for N and N.

Silence is kept

> God, you are love.
> Hold N and N in your love as they make their vows.

Bible Readings   **Remain in my love. Love one another as I have loved you**

As the Father has loved me, so I have loved you; abide in my love. If you keep my commandments, you will abide in my love, just as I have kept my Father's commandments and abide in his love. I have said these things to you so that my joy may be in you, and that your joy may be complete.

'This is my commandment, that you love one another as I have loved you. No one has greater love than this, to lay down one's life for one's friends. You are my friends if you do what I command you. I do not call you servants any longer, because the servant does not know what the master is doing; but I have called you friends, because I have made known to you everything that I have heard from my Father. You did not choose me but I chose you. And I appointed you to go and bear fruit, fruit that will last, so that the Father will give you whatever you ask him in my name. I am giving you these commands so that you may love one another.

John 15.9–17

Living in the spirit of trust and unity, through the joy and peace of God

We who are strong ought to put up with the failings of the weak, and not to please ourselves. Each of us must please our neighbour for the good purpose of building up the neighbour. For Christ did not please himself; but, as it is written, 'The insults of those who insult you have fallen on me.'

May the God of steadfastness and encouragement grant you to live in harmony with one another, in accordance with Christ Jesus, so that together you may with one voice glorify the God and Father of our Lord Jesus Christ.

Welcome one another, therefore, just as Christ has welcomed you, for the glory of God.

May the God of hope fill you with all joy and peace in believing, so that you may abound in hope by the power of the Holy Spirit.

Romans 15.1–3, 5–7, 13

As God's chosen people, clothe yourselves with compassion, kindness, humility, gentleness and patience

As God's chosen ones, holy and beloved, clothe yourselves with compassion, kindness, humility, meekness, and patience. Bear with one another and, if anyone has a complaint against another, forgive each other; just as the Lord has forgiven you, so you also must forgive. Above all, clothe yourselves with love, which binds everything together in perfect harmony. And let the peace of Christ rule in your hearts, to which indeed you were called in the one body. And be thankful. Let the word of Christ dwell in you richly; teach and admonish one another in all wisdom; and with gratitude in your hearts sing psalms, hymns, and spiritual songs to God. And whatever you do, in word or deed, do everything in the name of the Lord Jesus, giving thanks to God the Father through him.

Colossians 3.12–17

Other Readings   **True love**
Author unknown

True love is a sacred flame
That burns eternally,
And none can dim its special glow
Or change its destiny.
True love speaks in tender tones
And hears with gentle ear,
True love gives with open heart
And true love conquers fear.
True love makes no harsh demands
It neither rules nor binds,
And true love holds with gentle hands
The hearts that it entwines.

What is love?
Author unknown

Sooner or later we begin to understand that love is more than verses on valentines and romance in the movies. We begin to know that love is here and now, real and true, the most important thing in our lives. For love is the creator of our favourite memories and the foundation of our fondest dreams. Love is a promise that is always kept, a fortune that can never be spent, a seed that can flourish in even the most unlikely of places. And this radiance that never fades, this mysterious and magical joy, is the greatest treasure of all – one known only by those who love.

When you love someone
Anne Morrow Lindbergh
Extract from *Gift from the Sea*, published by Random House. This is available to view on the internet (see page x for copyright information).

The Blessing of the Marriage

Anyone who would like to is invited to come forward and lay hands in prayer on the couple as the minister prays

God, you are love and you created love.
Your Son Jesus died on the cross to show that love is the only true power.
Come now, Holy Spirit of God, and fill N and N with your love.
Bless them with a love for each other so strong that it will endure all things.
Make them people who love everyone.
Fill them now with trust in your love to guide their lives.
Amen

The people return to their seats

Prayers　　　　God of love, we give you thanks that in this marriage celebration N and N have committed their lives to each other. We pray
that their love will grow day by day as they journey through the
glad and sad times of the years ahead. We pray that your Holy
Spirit will guide them in the decisions they make. We pray that
they will have friends to share their journey and that, through
their love for each other, children will bless their lives.
Amen

*The congregation may be given cards and pens to write their own wishes and
blessings for the couple. (See templates of pew card designs on pages 141–43.)
These will be collected during the final hymn or song and placed in a basket on the
altar. They can later be given to the couple to keep. The minister says a prayer that
gathers up all the prayer requests*

The Blessing and Dismissal

After the blessing the minister says

N and N, go and celebrate the love that God has given you.
Then go to your home and live in that love.
Amen

Suggested Hymns　**Christ beside us**
and Songs　　　　(*Go Before Us*)

Let there be love shared among us
(*Complete Anglican Hymns Old and New*)

Love is the touch
(*One is the Body*)

Love one another
(*One is the Body*)

May the peace of the Lord Christ go with you
(*Celtic Hymn Book*)

The love we share
(*Hymns Old and New: One Church, One Faith, One Lord*)

Suggested Music	**A blessing** CD: *Fire of Love*, Margaret Rizza, Kevin Mayhew **Go forth into the world** CD: *Gloria and Other Sacred Music*, John Rutter, Hyperion **My companion** CD: *Celtic Roots & Rhythms 3 – Haven*, Nick and Anita Haigh, ICC (International Christian Communications)
Action	Cards, paper and a basket if wishes and blessings are to be written.

MARRIAGE SERVICE
WHEN A COUPLE HAVE
BEEN LIVING TOGETHER
AND HAVE CHILDREN

If a couple have been living together for some years and have children it is important that this is acknowledged in the marriage service. To ignore it is to pretend that
it has not happened. To acknowledge it is to celebrate what has gone before and to
bring it all together to offer to God as a new start and a new way forward for the
whole family. This service offers some ideas about how that might be done.

The Welcome   As we gather here today to witness the marriage of *N* and *N*,
                   may we all be filled with God's love.
                   God's love is for all of us,
                   We are God's precious children.
                   We thank God and welcome love.

Bible Readings   Love

                   If I speak in the tongues of mortals and of angels, but do not
                   have love, I am a noisy gong or a clanging cymbal. And if I
                   have prophetic powers, and understand all mysteries and all
                   knowledge, and if I have all faith, so as to remove mountains,
                   but do not have love, I am nothing. If I give away all my pos-
                   sessions, and if I hand over my body so that I may boast, but
                   do not have love, I gain nothing.
                       Love is patient; love is kind; love is not envious or boast-
                   ful or arrogant or rude. It does not insist on its own way; it

is not irritable or resentful; it does not rejoice in wrongdoing, but rejoices in the truth. It bears all things, believes all things, hopes all things, endures all things.

Love never ends. But as for prophecies, they will come to an end; as for tongues, they will cease; as for knowledge, it will come to an end. For we know only in part, and we prophesy only in part; but when the complete comes, the partial will come to an end. When I was a child, I spoke like a child, I thought like a child, I reasoned like a child; when I became an adult, I put an end to childish ways. For now we see in a mirror, dimly, but then we will see face to face. Now I know only in part; then I will know fully, even as I have been fully known. And now faith, hope, and love abide, these three; and the greatest of these is love.

1 Corinthians 13.1–13

Other Readings	**Breakfasting with the person you fell in love with**

Breakfasting with the person you fell in love with
Anne Morrow Lindbergh
Extract from *Gift from the Sea*, published by Random House. This is available to view on the internet (see page x for copyright information).

I am Love
Author unknown

Some say I can fly on the wind, yet I haven't any wings. Some have found me floating on the open sea, yet I cannot swim. Some have felt my warmth on cold nights, yet I have no flame. And though you cannot see me, I lay between two lovers at the hearth of fireplaces. I am the twinkle in your child's eyes. I am hidden in the lines of your mother's face. I am your father's shield as he guards your home. And yet ... Some say I am stronger than steel, yet I am as fragile as a tear. Some have never searched for me, yet I am around them always. Some say I die with loss, yet I am endless. And though you cannot hear me, I dance on the laughter of children. I am woven into the whispers of passion. I am in the blessings of grandmothers. I embrace the cries of newborn babies. And yet ... Some say I am a flower, yet I am also the seed. Some have little faith in me, yet I will always believe in them. Some say I cannot cure the ill, yet I nourish the soul. And though you cannot touch me, I am the gentle hand of the kind. I am the fingertips that caress your cheek at night. I am the hug of a child. I am Love.

Rite of Blessing the Family

The children join their parents, and the family and friends gather round in a circle holding hands – an unending circle of love holding the family in their midst. They all say together

> **N and N, and [*names of the children*], we stand here together surrounding you all with our love. We wish you much joy and rich blessings, and we pledge our support to you in your marriage.**

The Blessing of the Marriage

Father God, we thank you that you have brought N and N together today to declare their love for each other and exchange vows before you, their children and all their family and friends. We ask you to bless them as they continue their life together. May your love bind them together as they journey on. May they be filled with tenderness and love for each other, may they have generous open hearts, being aware of each other's needs, and the needs of others. May they be patient and loving parents to [*names of the children*], full of wisdom and understanding. May they share times of joy and laughter and, if the journey gets hard, may they know that they are your precious children and that you love them.
Amen

May you know deep love and companionship.
May you learn compromise and the gift to forgive each other.
May you be encircled by angels watching over you.
May the blessing of God, Father, Son and Holy Spirit, be upon you today and all through your life together.
Amen

The peace of the Lord be always with you.
And also with you.

Prayers

We thank God for all the gifts showered upon us,
for the coming together of N and N in marriage today,
for the privilege of being parents,
for families and friends gathered here to celebrate with them.
We all hold them in prayer and ask God's blessing upon them.
May the God of Love
be ever present in their lives.

May N and N know the joy of love.
May they grow ever closer as they journey through life together.
May their life be filled by the knowledge of God's love for them.
May the God of Love
be ever present in their lives.

As N and N journey on may they continue to build a home together that has an open door to welcome all,
a table spread with food to share,
and a generous spirit to those in need.
May the God of Love
be ever present in their lives.

We praise God and give thanks for the gift of children.
May N and N be wise and loving parents.
May they grow old together and watch their children and their children's children grow up.
May they journey to their life's end knowing and having known love.
May the God of Love
be ever present in their lives.

Suggested Hymns and Songs

Come on and celebrate
(*Complete Anglican Hymns Old and New*)

God, in the planning
(*Hymns Old and New: One Church, One Faith, One Lord*)

I will enter his gates
(*Songs of God's People*)

Jesus put this song into our hearts
(*Songs of Fellowship*)

O God, beyond all praising
(*Hymns Old and New: One Church, One Faith, One Lord*)

The grace of life is theirs
(*Hymns of Glory, Songs of Praise*)

Suggested Music   Faith, hope and love
CD: *Holy Gifts*, Stephen Dean, OCP Publications

I know you by heart
CD: *Songbird*, Eva Cassidy, Blix Street Records

Many are the lightbeams
CD: *Tales of Wonder*, Marty Haugen, GIA Publications

MARRIAGE SERVICE WHEN THE COUPLE ARE OLDER

When people meet later in life and want to marry it is important that the wedding service reflects where they are in their life's journey. It is hoped that the words used in this service will be helpful to those planning such a service.

The Welcome   We gather here today to witness the marriage of N and N. We have come to rejoice with them and give thanks to God that they have met each other along the road. We shall ask God to bless them as they journey on together as husband and wife. God's love embraces all of us.
We thank God and rejoice greatly!

The Preface

In the section of the Common Worship *Preface starting 'The gift of marriage brings husband and wife together' these new words might be used*

The gift of marriage brings husband and wife together in the delight and tenderness of sexual union and joyful commitment to the end of their lives.
It is there as a foundation on which to build love and trust, to offer love and support to each other in good times and bad, to bring companionship and comfort and to grow to maturity in love together.

Bible Reading   **The Road to Emmaus**

Now on that same day two of them were going to a village
called Emmaus, about seven miles from Jerusalem, and talking with each other about all these things that had happened.
While they were talking and discussing, Jesus himself came near
and went with them, but their eyes were kept from recognizing
him. And he said to them, 'What are you discussing with each
other while you walk along?' They stood still, looking sad.
Then one of them, whose name was Cleopas, answered him,
'Are you the only stranger in Jerusalem who does not know
the things that have taken place there in these days?' He asked
them, 'What things?' They replied, 'The things about Jesus of
Nazareth, who was a prophet mighty in deed and word before
God and all the people, and how our chief priests and leaders
handed him over to be condemned to death and crucified him.
But we had hoped that he was the one to redeem Israel. Yes,
and besides all this, it is now the third day since these things
took place. Moreover, some women of our group astounded
us. They were at the tomb early this morning, and when they
did not find his body there, they came back and told us that
they had indeed seen a vision of angels who said that he was
alive. Some of those who were with us went to the tomb and
found it just as the women had said; but they did not see him.'
Then he said to them, 'Oh, how foolish you are, and how slow
of heart to believe all that the prophets have declared! Was it
not necessary that the Messiah should suffer these things and
then enter into his glory?' Then beginning with Moses and all
the prophets, he interpreted to them the things about himself
in all the scriptures.

As they came near the village to which they were going,
he walked ahead as if he were going on. But they urged him
strongly, saying, 'Stay with us, because it is almost evening and
the day is now nearly over.' So he went in to stay with them.
When he was at the table with them, he took bread, blessed
and broke it, and gave it to them. Then their eyes were opened,
and they recognized him; and he vanished from their sight.
They said to each other, 'Were not our hearts burning within us
while he was talking to us on the road, while he was opening

the scriptures to us?' That same hour they got up and returned to Jerusalem; and they found the eleven and their companions gathered together. They were saying, 'The Lord has risen indeed, and he has appeared to Simon!' Then they told what had happened on the road, and how he had been made known to them in the breaking of the bread.

While they were talking about this, Jesus himself stood among them and said to them, 'Peace be with you.' They were startled and terrified, and thought that they were seeing a ghost. He said to them, 'Why are you frightened, and why do doubts arise in your hearts? Look at my hands and my feet; see that it is I myself. Touch me and see; for a ghost does not have flesh and bones as you see that I have.' And when he had said this, he showed them his hands and his feet. While in their joy they were disbelieving and still wondering, he said to them, 'Have you anything here to eat?' They gave him a piece of broiled fish, and he took it and ate in their presence.

Then he said to them, 'These are my words that I spoke to you while I was still with you – that everything written about me in the law of Moses, the prophets, and the psalms must be fulfilled.'

Luke 24.13–44

Other Readings   **Adapted from *Far from the Madding Crowd***
Thomas Hardy

We are all on our own paths, all on our own journeys.
Sometimes the paths cross, and people arrive at the crossing points at the same time and meet each other.
There are greetings, pleasantries are exchanged, and then they move on.
But then once in a while the pleasantries become more, friendship grows, deeper links are made, hands are joined and love flies.
The friendship has turned into love.
Paths are joined, one path with two people walking it, both going in the same direction, and sharing each other's journeys.
Today N and N are joining their paths.
They will now skip together in harmony and love, sharing joys

and sorrows, hopes and fears, strengthening and upholding each other as they walk along side by side.

At home by the fire, whenever I look up, there you will be. And whenever you look up, there I shall be.

The Rite of Encircling the Couple with Love

All the family and friends gather round the couple in a circle. The circle is to symbolize their love and support for the newly married couple. They all say together

A circle has no beginning and no end, which is why we symbolically stand here in a circle, to show to you both our never-ending love and support. We pledge to continue to uphold you in your journey together. We wish you much joy, rich blessings and deep contentment in your marriage. Amen

The Blessing of the Marriage

May hands joined,
vows spoken,
and rings exchanged
lead you to a life together of deep commitment,
shared joys, tenderness and peace.

The blessing of God,
Father, Son and Holy Spirit
be with you as you start this new journey together.
Amen

The peace of the Lord be always with you.
And also with you.

Everyone exchanges a greeting and returns to their seats

Prayers   We give thanks to God that N and N met each other as they walked their paths through life. We give thanks that they have found love one for the other and today have declared before God, and all of us gathered here, that they wish to continue their journey together with God's blessing upon them.

God's blessing be upon the bride and groom.
Lord, lighten their path and guide them on their way.

May N and N have a joyful life together.
May they be blessed with years of happiness, full of the knowledge of God walking the road with them.
May they show patience, understanding and tenderness, being aware of each other's needs, as they grow together in trusting love.

God's blessing be upon the bride and groom.
Lord, lighten their path and guide them on their way.

In the reading we heard that Cleopas and his friend urged Jesus to stay and have a meal with them, may N and N also welcome people into their home. May there be generosity and awareness of the other in the way they lead their lives. May their home be warm and welcoming, offering hospitality and refreshment to all who cross the threshold.

God's blessing be upon the bride and groom.
Lord, lighten their path and guide them on their way.

As Jesus walked along the road towards Emmaus he joined in the conversation that Cleopas was having with his friend. He took time to listen to their worries and helped them to understand. May N and N give time to their family and friends, being aware of their needs, celebrating in times of joy and offering solace in times of sadness.

God's blessing be upon the bride and groom.
Lord, lighten their path and guide them on their way.

The Dismissal and Blessing

May the entwining of your journeys today lead to a time of deep joy, harmony and contentment;
and may the blessing of God almighty,
the Father, the Son, and the Holy Spirit,
be with you and all whom you love,
today and always.
Amen

Suggested Hymns and Songs

God of life be with you
(*Celtic Hymn Book*)

Let love be real
(*Liturgical Hymns Old and New*)

Lord, for the years
(*Hymns Old and New: New Anglican Edition*)

Love divine, all loves excelling
(*Hymns Old and New: New Anglican Edition*)

May the Lord bless you
(*Be Still and Know*)

Now thank we all our God
(*Hymns Old and New: New Anglican Edition*)

Suggested Music

A Clare benediction
CD: *Gloria and Other Sacred Music*, John Rutter, Hyperion Records

Fand
CD: *Celtic Heartbeat*, Maire Breatnach, Demon Music Group Ltd

Love one another
CD: *Take this Moment*, The Cathedral Singers, GIA Publications

MARRIAGE SERVICE IN CHURCH AFTER DIVORCE

Here is a suggestion from Ann Lewin for an introduction to a marriage service after a divorce. It is from her book *Words by the Way: Ideas and Resources for Use Throughout the Christian Year* (published by Inspire and copyright © Ann Lewin 2005) and is reproduced here with her permission.

With the bride and groom standing at the front of the church, facing each other but apart, the minister addresses the congregation

> N and N have come to celebrate their marriage, (each) with memories of a previous relationship. They want, as they prepare to make their vows to each other, to give thanks for all that was good in those partnerships (*especially their children), to acknowledge responsibility for their own part in the breakdown of their first marriage, and to ask forgiveness for their own personal failures to live in love.

Addressing N and N

> N and N, you have talked with each other, and faced as honestly as you can the reasons for the breakdown of your previous relationships. Each of you is loved by God, and nothing you have done has put you beyond that love. You, like all of us, need assurance that God's love is greater than our failures, and I invite you now to open yourselves again to the healing power of God's forgiveness.**

Silence

We say together
Compassionate God,
come to us and heal us;
forgive our failures to love,
and free us from guilt
about what is past.
Help us to love and serve you
wholeheartedly
in our new relationship
with each other.

God in his mercy sets us free.
Take hold of this forgiveness
and live your lives together
in joy and freedom in God's love.
Amen

*   Omit if there are no children.
** At this point the minister could add something along these lines:

> N and N have identified their particular need, but we all stand in need
> of forgiveness, and all of us can join in these words, whether aloud or in
> our hearts, and receive God's forgiveness.

MARRIAGE SERVICE AFTER THE DEATH OF A PARTNER OR PARTNERS

Here are some resources for a situation where two people want to get married whose past includes the bereavement of one or both previous partners. We have provided a Rite of Remembering. The minister might tell the congregation that N and N have met and fallen in love since the death(s) of *N/N's wife/husband*. The minister suggests that nothing can take away or replace the precious memories and stories of past years, but that these will be woven into the stories of the years that are to come. This is but a new chapter in the stories of N and N and is a day for rejoicing and celebration. The minister particularly welcomes the children of any previous marriage(s).

The Welcome   Heavenly Father, your love has gathered us in this place to celebrate and witness the marriage of N and N. They will declare their love for each other and make their marriage vows. We rejoice with them as they begin a new life together. Send your Holy Spirit on your people and fill our hearts with love and joy and thanksgiving. We ask this in Jesus' name.
Amen

The Rite of Remembering a Spouse who has Died

After the Declarations there may be a Rite of Remembering and acknowledgement of a previous marriage or marriages beginning with the following reading

Bible Reading	**They are like angels in heaven**

The same day some Sadducees came to him, saying there is no resurrection; and they asked him a question, saying, 'Teacher, Moses said, "If a man dies childless, his brother shall marry the widow, and raise up children for his brother." Now there were seven brothers among us; the first married, and died childless, leaving the widow to his brother. The second did the same, so also the third, down to the seventh. Last of all, the woman herself died. In the resurrection, then, whose wife of the seven will she be? For all of them had married her.'

Jesus answered them, 'You are wrong, because you know neither the scriptures nor the power of God. For in the resurrection they neither marry nor are given in marriage, but are like angels in heaven.'

Matthew 22.23–30

The bereaved bride or groom prays

God of life,
I thank you for my blessed years of marriage to N.
I thank you for your grace that enabled us to keep our promises,
in sickness and in health, till death us did part.
I thank you for the wisdom from our marriage
that I now offer in my new marriage to N.
By your Holy Spirit I now leave N in your safe keeping for ever,
held in your boundless love.

She/he then gives to the minister a photo of N and, if available, a ring(s) from that former marriage and says

For me the time with N is now past.
My life is now with N,
but all is held in your one love, O Lord.

The minister puts the 'items of memory' in an unobtrusive place, just visible but away from the focus of the service

The other bride or groom now prays

> As I take N to be my *wife/husband*,
> I take all that *she/he* is.
> I take all *her/his* memories
> and promise to honour them.
> I will comfort *her/him* in times of grief.
> Holy Spirit, you are called Comforter and wise Counsellor,
> help us in this mystery of love that is greater than death.

The bride and groom are handed a small bunch of flowers each. They are each given a ribbon of a different colour. They then tie the two bunches of flowers into one, using their ribbons. Holding the flowers together, they place them in front of the 'items of memory'. Standing together by that place, they say together after the minister

> We thank you, Lord, for that former marriage
> that is now complete with you.
> Lead us forward in our new marriage,
> as we honour all that is in each other's hearts.

All can be repeated if both the bride and groom's former spouses have died. The final prayer would be said together, changing the first two lines to plural

(If the former spouse(s) is buried in the churchyard where the marriage is taking place, the couple, or a family member, may now go and place the flowers on that grave. While they do this a hymn may be sung, for example 'Now thank we all our God' or 'Lord, for the years'. Or this may be done at the end of the service)

Bible Readings   **The Beatitudes**

When Jesus saw the crowds, he went up the mountain; and after he sat down, his disciples came to him. Then he began to speak, and taught them, saying:

'Blessed are the poor in spirit, for theirs is the kingdom of heaven.

'Blessed are those who mourn, for they will be comforted.

'Blessed are the meek, for they will inherit the earth.

'Blessed are those who hunger and thirst for righteousness, for they will be filled.

'Blessed are the merciful, for they will receive mercy.

'Blessed are the pure in heart, for they will see God.

'Blessed are the peacemakers, for they will be called children of God.

'Blessed are those who are persecuted for righteousness' sake, for theirs is the kingdom of heaven.

'Blessed are you when people revile you and persecute you and utter all kinds of evil against you falsely on my account. Rejoice and be glad, for your reward is great in heaven, for in the same way they persecuted the prophets who were before.'

Matthew 5.1–12

Love

If I speak in the tongues of mortals and of angels, but do not have love, I am a noisy gong or a clanging cymbal. And if I have prophetic powers, and understand all mysteries and all knowledge, and if I have all faith, so as to remove mountains, but do not have love, I am nothing. If I give away all my possessions, and if I hand over my body so that I may boast, but do not have love, I gain nothing.

Love is patient; love is kind; love is not envious or boastful or arrogant or rude. It does not insist on its own way; it is not irritable or resentful; it does not rejoice in wrongdoing, but rejoices in the truth. It bears all things, believes all things, hopes all things, endures all things.

Love never ends. But as for prophecies, they will come to an end; as for tongues, they will cease; as for knowledge, it will come to an end. For we know only in part, and we prophesy only in part; but when the complete comes, the partial will come to an end. When I was a child, I spoke like a child, I thought like a child, I reasoned like a child; when I became an adult, I put an end to childish ways. For now we see in a mirror, dimly, but then we will see face to face. Now I know only in part; then I will know fully, even as I have been fully known. And now faith, hope, and love abide, these three; and the greatest of these is love.

1 Corinthians 13.1–13

Love one another, for love is from God

Beloved, let us love one another, because love is from God; everyone who loves is born of God and knows God. Whoever does not love does not know God, for God is love. God's love was revealed among us in this way: God sent his only Son into the world so that we might live through him. In this is love, not that we loved God but that he loved us and sent his Son to be the atoning sacrifice for our sins. Beloved, since God loved us so much, we also ought to love one another. No one has ever seen God; if we love one another, God lives in us, and his love is perfected in us.

1 John 4.7–12

Other Readings   **A walled garden**
Author unknown

Your marriage should have within it a secret and protected space, open to you alone. Imagine it to be a walled garden, entered by a door to which you only hold the key. Within this garden you will cease to be a mother, father, employee, home-maker or any other of the roles which you fulfil in daily life. Here you can be yourselves, two people who love each other. Here you can concentrate on one another's needs. So take each other's hands and go forth to your garden. The time you spend together is not wasted but invested – invested in your future and nurture of your love.

The blessing of the Apaches
Author unknown

Now you will feel no rain
For each of you will be shelter to the other.
Now you will feel no cold
For each of you will be warmth to the other.
Now there is no more loneliness for you
For each of you will be companion to the other.
Now you are two bodies
But there is only one life before you.
Go now to your dwelling place

To enter into the days of your togetherness
And may your days be good, and long, upon the earth.

To be at one with each other
George Eliot

What greater thing is there for two human souls than to feel
that they are joined – to strengthen each other – to be at one
with each other in silent unspeakable memories.

Prayers

God of love, we give you thanks that N and N have declared
their love and made their vows together in your presence. In
their love for each other we may glimpse that love which is
eternal and which you freely give to all people.
God of love, hear our prayer.

God of joy, we pray that your Holy Spirit will live in N and
N as they journey through life, filling them with a sense of
adventure. May their faith remain strong and true. May the
joy which is present here today surround them in all the years
to come.
God of joy, hear our prayer.

God of compassion, we remember those we have loved who
have died, and who are now alive with you in the company of
all your saints. May N and N cherish memories of past years
while knowing, too, that the love they have now found together is good, and of God.
God of compassion, hear our prayer.

God of hope, we pray that the lives of N and N will be filled
with grace. We pray that their home may be a place of welcome
and hospitality, where children, families and friends will share
the love which they have found.
God of hope, hear our prayer.

**The Blessing
and Dismissal**

May God fill your lives with love, joy, compassion and hope in
abundance. May you go forth from this place in peace to live
in harmony with all people, and may the blessing of God the

Father, God the Son and God the Holy Spirit be with you this day, and in all the days to come.
Amen

Suggested Hymns and Songs

A new commandment
(*Complete Anglican Hymns Old and New*)

At the heart of all things
(*New Start Hymns and Songs*)

Living God, your word has called us
(*New Start Hymns and Songs*)

Through all the changing scenes of life
(*Hymns Old and New: New Anglican Edition*)

When love is found
(*Laudate*)

You shall go out with joy
(*Songs of God's People*)

Suggested Music

Gathered in the love of Christ (Canon in D)
CD: *The Song and the Silence*, Marty Haugen, GIA Publications

I am the Light of the World
CD: *God's Eye is on the Sparrow*, Bob Hurd and Anawim, OCP Publications

Perhaps love
CD: *A Song's Best Friend: The Very Best of John Denver*, BMG

Action

Two small bunches of flowers.

Two different coloured ribbons.

A photograph/s of the deceased person/s.

Ring(s) from the previous marriage(s).

ORDER FOR A MARRIAGE SERVICE WITHIN A CELEBRATION OF HOLY COMMUNION

The Gathering

The Welcome
Prayers of Penitence
Preface
The Declarations
The Collect

The Liturgy of the Word

Readings
Gospel Reading
Sermon

The Marriage

The Vows
The Giving of Rings
The Proclamation
The Blessing of the Marriage

Registration of the Marriage

Prayers

The Liturgy of the Sacrament

The Peace

Preparation of the Table

The Eucharistic Prayer

The Lord's Prayer

The Blessing of the Marriage

Breaking of the Bread

Giving of Communion

Prayer after Communion

The Dismissal

MARRIAGE SERVICE WITHIN A CELEBRATION OF HOLY COMMUNION

When there is Holy Communion in a service it usually indicates that the couple getting married have an established faith and that they feel that their guests are also able to join them in receiving the bread and the wine. It might be that the couple would like to give the bread and wine to each other. This will be their first meal together as a married couple and acts as a symbolic reminder that Christ will be with them every time they share a meal together or welcome others to join them at their table in years to come.

The Welcome	In the name of God who loves you as *his/her* precious child, in the name of Jesus who shows us love and freedom, in the name of the Holy Spirit who gives us inspiration, welcome!
	We are gathered here today to witness the marriage of N and N. We shall be witnesses as they exchange solemn vows. We shall commit ourselves to support them in their marriage. We shall share bread and wine, broken and given to us all in love. We shall go out filled with joy, for this is the day the Lord has made. **We shall rejoice and be very glad in it.**
Bible Readings	**The lovers celebrate the joy of creation** My beloved speaks and says to me: 'Arise, my love, my fair one,

and come away;
for now the winter is past,
the rain is over and gone.
The flowers appear on the earth;
the time of singing has come,
and the voice of the turtle-dove
is heard in our land.
The fig tree puts forth its figs,
and the vines are in blossom;
they give forth fragrance.
Arise, my love, my fair one,
and come away.

The Song of Solomon 2.10–13

The house built on sure foundations

'Everyone then who hears these words of mine and acts on them will be like a wise man who built his house on rock. The rain fell, the floods came, and the winds blew and beat on that house, but it did not fall, because it had been founded on rock. And everyone who hears these words of mine and does not act on them will be like a foolish man who built his house on sand. The rain fell, and the floods came, and the winds blew and beat against that house, and it fell – and great was its fall!'

Matthew 7.24–27

The true vine

'I am the true vine, and my Father is the vine-grower. He removes every branch in me that bears no fruit. Every branch that bears fruit he prunes to make it bear more fruit.'

John 15.1–2

Other Readings   **Love is**
Tessa Wilkinson

Love is
… to wait with anticipation for the key in the door
… to walk down the street with fingers entwined

... to laugh until the tears pour down your cheeks
... to stand together in awe and wonder when something
   beautiful is shared
... to journey with a spirit of expectation
... to rise above exhaustion
... to always give that little bit more
... to always forgive and start again
... to know total togetherness and at the same time total
   freedom
Love flies, love runs, love leaps for joy
Love lights a dark place
Love welcomes
Love transforms
Those who love are richly blessed

Today N and N are welcoming love into their lives.
May their eyes be open to the beauty around them.
May they be given the strength to cope with all they encounter
as they journey together.
May they share joys and sorrows, hopes and fears.
And may they strengthen and uphold each other as they walk
along side by side.

The Proclamation

Before the service everyone is given a 'party-popper'. When the couple are declared to be man and wife the poppers are let off and everyone cheers. This gives a wonderful sense of celebration

The Blessing of the Marriage

May love ...
surround you both,
hold you on your journey,
be the welcome at your door,
be at the centre of your home and family,
be between you and all whom you meet.
Go well, with love in your hearts

and at the centre of all you do.
And the blessing of God Almighty,
Father, Son and Holy Spirit be upon you both,
today and always.
Amen

Prayers

Preparation of the Table

It is good to reflect on who might bring up the gifts. It might be parents or grand-parents, best friends, or someone who has played an important role in the lives of the bride and groom. It is an opportunity to involve more people in having a special role during the service

Candle Lighting

There is now an opportunity for the bride and groom and their parents to symboli-cally pass the light of parenthood over to the newly married couple, showing that the time of being a 'child' is passed and the new time of marriage is beginning. Each set of parents lights a candle which they carry together to their child. (See 'How to Put a Design on to a Candle' on page 131.) The bride and groom each hold an unlit candle and their parents light these candles from their candles. The parents then say

> **We pass this light from us to you, as your journey with us ends and your new journey with N begins.**
> **Go out from here with the Light of Christ showing you the way.**

The bride and groom then turn and light a single candle from their candles, mak-ing one light. As they light the one candle they say together

> **We thank God for the life our parents have given us.**
> **We ask God's blessing on them today.**
> **As we start our new life together we pray that the Light of Christ will shine in our hearts and in our lives.**
> **Amen**

**The Dismissal
and Blessing**

See above

**Suggested Hymns
and Songs**

Be still, for the presence of the Lord
(*Complete Anglican Hymns Old and New*)

Come on and celebrate
(*Complete Anglican Hymns Old and New*)

God, whose love is all around us
(*Be Still and Know*)

Let's praise the Creator who gave us each other
(*Hymns of Glory, Songs of Praise*)

Put peace into each other's hands
(*Hymns of Glory, Songs of Praise*)

Such love
(*Complete Anglican Hymns Old and New*)

We come, dear Lord, to celebrate
(*Hymns of Glory, Songs of Praise*)

You are the vine
(*Songs of Fellowship*)

Suggested Music

A Celtic blessing
CD: *Light in our Darkness*, Margaret Rizza, Kevin Mayhew

I am the vine
CD: *God's Eye is on the Sparrow*, Bob Hurd and Anawim, OCP Publications

Send us forth
CD: *God's Eye is on the Sparrow*, Bob Hurd and Anawim, OCP Publications

Take my gifts
CD: *Go Before Us*, Bernadette Farrell, OCP Publications

Action

Five candles are needed – one for each set of parents, one each for the bride and groom, and one for the couple to light.

Party-poppers to let off at the Proclamation.

Make a stole with two candles on it (see 'How to Make a Stole' on page 121 and template of candle designs on page 125).

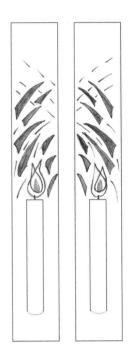

PART THREE: THANKSGIVING FOR MARRIAGE AND RENEWAL OF MARRIAGE VOWS

ORDER FOR THANKSGIVING FOR MARRIAGE

Introduction

The Welcome
Prayer of Preparation
Preface
Readings
Sermon

Renewal of Vows

The Rings
Prayers
The Dismissal

RENEWAL OF MARRIAGE VOWS FOR MORE THAN ONE COUPLE

A situation when a renewal of marriage vows for multiple couples is planned has to be very carefully thought out. If held within a normal Sunday service, a large proportion of the congregation who may not be married, or whose marriages have ended because of bereavement, or ended because of grief of another sort, will feel excluded. It may be better to plan a special service at a different time, inviting all those who would like to renew their vows to come. The renewal of vows could take place within a celebration of Holy Communion or as part of an evening Songs of Praise, where the couples have chosen their favourite hymns.

This might be at the end of a Celebration of Marriage Weekend in the parish. Place chunky candles on the altar – one for each couple. Each candle will have written on it 'The Light of Christ' and the names of the couple. A ribbon is tied around the bottom of each candle. Next to each candle is a small prayer card with the words the couple are to speak (see below). The Paschal Candle is lit and placed near the altar.

The same resources could of course be adjusted and used for just one couple.

The Welcome   This is the day the Lord has made!
Let us rejoice and be glad in it!

Welcome! You have come to this holy place together to renew your wedding vows.
We give thanks for the time that has passed, and look forward with faith to the time that lies ahead.
We give thanks for the love which God has, in his goodness, showered upon you, and we look forward to that same love surrounding you as you journey on together.

We give thanks that God has drawn you to this place, and that you may now, in his presence, and in the presence of your families and friends, renew the sacred vows that you made at your marriages.

The grace of our Lord Jesus Christ,
and the love of God,
and the fellowship of the Holy Spirit
be with you all evermore.
And also with you.

Bible Readings

The Wedding at Cana

On the third day there was a wedding in Cana of Galilee, and the mother of Jesus was there. Jesus and his disciples had also been invited to the wedding. When the wine gave out, the mother of Jesus said to him, 'They have no wine.' And Jesus said to her, 'Woman, what concern is that to you and to me? My hour has not yet come.' His mother said to the servants, 'Do whatever he tells you.' Now standing there were six stone water-jars for the Jewish rites of purification, each holding twenty or thirty gallons. Jesus said to them, 'Fill the jars with water.' And they filled them up to the brim. He said to them, 'Now draw some out, and take it to the chief steward.' So they took it. When the steward tasted the water that had become wine, and did not know where it came from (though the servants who had drawn the water knew), the steward called the bridegroom and said to him, 'Everyone serves the good wine first, and then the inferior wine after the guests have become drunk. But you have kept the good wine until now.' Jesus did this, the first of his signs, in Cana of Galilee, and revealed his glory; and his disciples believed in him.

John 2.1–11

Love

If I speak in the tongues of mortals and of angels, but do not have love, I am a noisy gong or a clanging cymbal. And if I have prophetic powers, and understand all mysteries and all knowledge, and if I have all faith, so as to remove mountains, but do not have love, I am nothing. If I give away all my possessions, and if I hand over my body so that I may boast, but do not have love, I gain nothing.

Love is patient; love is kind; love is not envious or boastful or arrogant or rude. It does not insist on its own way; it is not irritable or resentful; it does not rejoice in wrongdoing, but rejoices in the truth. It bears all things, believes all things, hopes all things, endures all things.

Love never ends. But as for prophecies, they will come to an end; as for tongues, they will cease; as for knowledge, it will come to an end. For we know only in part, and we prophesy only in part; but when the complete comes, the partial will come to an end. When I was a child, I spoke like a child, I thought like a child, I reasoned like a child; when I became an adult, I put an end to childish ways. For now we see in a mirror, dimly, but then we will see face to face. Now I know only in part; then I will know fully, even as I have been fully known. And now faith, hope, and love abide, these three; and the greatest of these is love.

1 Corinthians 13.1–13

Other Readings   From *This Sunrise of Wonder*
Michael Mayne

There is the mystery of the relationship between two persons: what the marriage service in the Prayer Book calls 'the mystery of one flesh', a man and a woman who, through growing together by the daily unspoken giving and receiving of love in small ways, find that over the years each has been invaded and shaped by the reality of the other, in a way that does not diminish, but rather enhances, each of them.
(pages 17–18)

Adapted from *This Sunrise of Wonder*
Michael Mayne

Falling in love *(is a cause for wonder)*, especially when that leads to a deep and lifelong commitment; and to give yourself without reserve to that particular mystery is to trust that you are able to be lifted out of the narrowness of self in the give-

and-take of love, and in so transcending yourself become more, not less, what you truly are.
(page 52)

Renewal of Vows

The couples come forward to the altar and receive a taper. Then each couple, holding the taper together, take light from the Paschal Candle and light their candle on the altar. They pick up their card and, and facing the congregation, say

> **May the light of Christ shine on us as we now make our vows, and may we reflect this light as we go from this place to continue our marriage together.**

The couples then reaffirm their marriage vows and return to their seats

The Rings

The minister asks the couples to face each other as rings are blessed and commitments given. The couples may kiss and the families and friends may clap

Prayers

Almighty God, our heavenly Father,
you have blessed your people with the gift of marriage.
Be with us now and fill us with your Holy Spirit,
that each marriage covenant renewed here today will be a faithful sign of your love in the world.
Gathered in your love, we pray.

We pray for our families and friends.
May we hold fast to the love that we share and may we celebrate together in times of joy, and comfort one another in times of sorrow.
Gathered in your love, we pray.

We pray for our homes.
May our homes be places where friends, and strangers, are made welcome, where bread is broken and wine is poured, and where stories are shared and enjoyed.
Gathered in your love, we pray.

We pray for your troubled world.
May the love that we have for each other, so abundant in this place here today, overflow into the world around us, filling it with your light.
Gathered in your love, we pray.

We pray for the years ahead.
May we grow in grace, knowing your presence with us and, at the end of our earthly lives, may we be welcomed to your marriage feast in heaven, with all your saints and angels.
Gathered in your love, we pray.

The Blessing and Dismissal

Go out into the world
with hopes and dreams renewed
to live and love in the peace of God.
With the help of God, we will.
Amen

Suggested Hymns and Songs

Lord, for the years
(*Hymns Old and New: New Anglican Edition*)

Lord of our growing years
(*Hymns of Glory, Songs of Praise*)

Love divine, all loves excelling
(*Hymns Old and New: New Anglican Edition*)

Through all the changing scenes of life
(*Hymns Old and New: New Anglican Edition*)

Where the love of Christ unites us
(*Celtic Hymn Book*)

Your love, O God, has called us here
(*Hymns of Glory, Songs of Praise*)

Suggested Music

Cantate Domino canticum novum
CD: *Christe Lux Mundi*, Taizé Community, GIA Publications

Celebration
CD: *Dreamcatcher*, Secret Garden, Philips

Christ beside us
CD: *Go Before Us*, Bernadette Farrell, OCP Publications

Action   Tapers, ribbon and chunky candles are needed for each couple. The words on the candles can either be written straight onto the candles with a pen or the words can be printed on sticky labels and stuck on. (See 'How to Put a Design on to a Candle' on page 131.)

Small cards with words on for each couple to place by each candle. (See templates for card designs on page 140.)

Put the name of the couple here

MAY THE LIGHT OF CHRIST SHINE ON US
AS WE NOW MAKE OUR VOWS,
AND MAY WE REFLECT THIS LIGHT
AS WE GO FROM THIS PLACE TO
CONTINUE OUR MARRIAGE TOGETHER.

MAY THE LIGHT OF CHRIST
SHINE ON US AS WE NOW
MAKE OUR VOWS, AND
MAY WE REFLECT THIS
LIGHT AS WE GO FROM
THIS PLACE TO CONTINUE
OUR MARRIAGE TOGETHER.

RENEWAL OF MARRIAGE VOWS AFTER A TIME OF SEPARATION OR DIFFICULTY

When a couple have been through a difficult time in their marriage and they have decided to make a fresh start they might like to renew their marriage vows. This can be done in a simple way that can be part of a normal Sunday service, or they might like to have a separate service, quietly on their own or with their family present. The advantage of renewing vows in a Sunday service is that not only their family, but also the church family, will be there and can agree to support them as they declare their intention to try to start again. The point at which this takes place in the service can be decided to suit the church. To make the couple feel that there is real recognition of what they are doing, it would be good to speak to them before the event to see if there is anything they would particularly like to include in the service. This might include choosing a hymn that they had at their wedding, or choosing the flowers or the colour scheme in the church. It is an opportunity for everyone to share the good news together. Cake and a drink might be served at the end of the service.

The Welcome We are going to pause in the service for a moment to reflect on God's wonderful gift of marriage. Being married is not always easy, and N and N have been going though a very difficult time recently when their marriage became very fragile. I am delighted to say that after much soul searching they have decided to renew their marriage vows and to make a fresh start together.

This is something that we can all rejoice in and celebrate together. Often it seems much easier to give up on a marriage than to work on its healing. The work to rebuild something that seems to have ended can seem a very long, hard road. But *N* and *N* are determined to start again. To succeed they will need not only each other, but also their family and friends. They will need to be surrounded by love and support, and everyone here today can help in that.

So before we ask them to renew their vows I want to ask you all:

Will you agree to uphold *N* and *N* in their renewed marriage, supporting them in every way you can and helping them to find joy and happiness together?
We will.

The couple can be asked to come out to the front of the church

There is now a time to reflect on what has gone wrong and to ask God's forgiveness

God is a loving God who wants us to love one another. Over and over again God offers us forgiveness and the opportunity to start afresh. Let us all reflect in a moment of silence and think of the many things we have got wrong, the pain we have caused to others and the things we regret.

Do you acknowledge the pain you have caused to each other, and do you ask God forgiveness?
We do, and ask God to forgive us.

The minister then turns to the couple

Minister to couple	When times get hard, things can be said in anger that can hurt and need to be healed.
Couple to each other	**I am sorry, please forgive me.**
Minister to couple	When times get hard, events can happen that we regret.
Couple to each other	**I am sorry, please forgive me.**
Minister to couple	When times get hard, the way we behave can impact on family and friends.
Couple to everyone present	**We are sorry, please forgive us.**

Each situation is different and the couple need to think whether there are particular people from whom they need to seek forgiveness. They might face them in turn to say 'Sorry'

Minister to couple   God forgives you both, and blesses you both, and rejoices with you both as you start again together.

The couple can now renew their vows and rededicate their rings

So let us praise God for the gift of marriage!

We are told that marriage is a gift of God and that the purpose of marriage is that the couple should give themselves to each other, that they should comfort and help each other, and live faithfully together in need and in plenty, in joy and in sorrow, and that it is a way of life that should be honoured by all.
We thank God that *N* and *N* have rededicated their marriage vows and intend to live their lives with their marriage at the heart of all they do.

Minister to couple   May you go in peace together, reunited in love for each other, to find God's joy in all you do.
Amen

The couple return to their seats and the service continues

RENEWAL OF MARRIAGE VOWS FOR A SIGNIFICANT ANNIVERSARY

When a couple come to a significant anniversary, it is a wonderful opportunity for the church family to celebrate with them and their family simply in the context of a normal Sunday service. The minister can decide the appropriate place in the service where this can happen. To make the couple feel that there is real recognition of what they have achieved, it might be good to speak to them before the event to see if there is anything they would particularly like to include in the service. This might include choosing a hymn that they had at their wedding, or choosing the flowers or the colour scheme in the church. It is an opportunity for everyone to share some cake and a drink at the end of the service.

The Welcome

The couple can be asked to come out to the front of the church

We are going to pause in the service for a moment to reflect on God's wonderful gift of marriage and to give God thanks and praise for the *xx* years that N and N have spent together.
Marriage is not always an easy journey, the pathway can sometimes become steep and rugged, but with love at the heart of it those 'steep pathway' moments can soon be turned to places where the couple can skip along together again.
So let us praise God for the gift of marriage!

If the couple wish, they can be invited to say something about their marriage – how they met, when they married, their wedding day, and maybe a little about their journey together. This will give those who do not know them more of a picture of what is being celebrated

We are told that marriage is a gift of God and that the purpose of marriage is that the couple should give themselves to each other, that they should comfort and help each other, and live faithfully together in need and in plenty, in joy and in sorrow, and that it is a way of life that should be honoured by all.

We thank God that N and N dedicated their marriage to God for this purpose *xx* years ago.

On this anniversary day we pray that they will be strengthened and guided by God through the rest of their lives together.

We will all continue to honour and support them in that endeavour.

Bible Reading   Love

If I speak in the tongues of mortals and of angels, but do not have love, I am a noisy gong or a clanging cymbal. And if I have prophetic powers, and understand all mysteries and all knowledge, and if I have all faith, so as to remove mountains, but do not have love, I am nothing. If I give away all my possessions, and if I hand over my body so that I may boast, but do not have love, I gain nothing.

Love is patient; love is kind; love is not envious or boastful or arrogant or rude. It does not insist on its own way; it is not irritable or resentful; it does not rejoice in wrongdoing, but rejoices in the truth. It bears all things, believes all things, hopes all things, endures all things.

Love never ends. But as for prophecies, they will come to an end; as for tongues, they will cease; as for knowledge, it will come to an end. For we know only in part, and we prophesy only in part; but when the complete comes, the partial will come to an end. When I was a child, I spoke like a child, I thought like a child, I reasoned like a child; when I became an adult, I put an end to childish ways. For now we see in a mirror, dimly, but then we will see face to face. Now I know only in part; then I will know fully, even as I have been fully known.

And now faith, hope, and love abide, these three; and the greatest of these is love.

1 Corinthians 13.1–13

Renewal of vows

The couple might like to renew their vows. These can be the vows they said to each other on their wedding day, or they might write something new that they would like to say to each other

The Ring

The couple might like to rededicate their rings, or dedicate new ones

Prayers

If the reading has been from 1 Corinthians 13, these prayers might be used. They might be read by two people, one saying what love is, the other saying the prayers

Voice One	In the reading from Corinthians we hear that: Love is patient.
Voice Two	Help us to be patient and always be prepared to go on a little bit longer than we want to, Lord.
Voice One	Love is kind.
Voice Two	Help us to put kindness at the heart of all we do.
Voice One	Love does not envy.
Voice Two	Lord, rather than wanting more, help us to look at the many things we already have and be grateful for them.
Voice One	Love does not boast.
Voice Two	Lord, if there are things that we are good at, help us to use them to further your kingdom, and not to brag about them for our own gratification.

Voice One	Love is not proud.
Voice Two	Lord, help us in moments when we feel arrogant and superior to remember that we are all your precious children and that none of us is more important than any other, and that you love us all equally.
Voice One	Love is not rude.
Voice Two	Lord, we know we can so easily be rude or impolite, especially when we want things done 'our way'. We so often fail to be patient and kind. Father, forgive us.
Voice One	Love is not self-seeking.
Voice Two	Lord, we are so good at putting ourselves first. We can so easily be the centre of all we do, being absorbed in what we think is important, showing no interest in those around us. Help us to turn away from ourselves and become aware of the needs of others.
Voice One	Love is not easily angered.
Voice Two	Lord, when we feel anger welling up in us, and we want to scream and shout, help us to turn our anger to love.
Voice One	Love keeps no record of wrongs.
Voice Two	Lord, we know you will always forgive us, whatever we do. Help us to live our lives forgiving others as you have forgiven us.
All	**May we walk as children of love,** **striving at all times to do better** **and praising God for the blessings showered upon us.**
The Blessing and Dismissal	May *we/you* go out into the world warmed with the joy of this day. May God's love surround *us/you*. May God's peace be in *our/your* hearts. May the peace of the Lord be upon *us/you* and all whom *we/you* love. **Let us all go from here filled with the light and love of Christ.** **Amen**

Suggested Hymns and Songs	**Lord, for the years** (*Hymns Old and New: New Anglican Edition*) **Lord of our growing years** (*Hymns of Glory, Songs of Praise*) **Love is patient** (*Celtic Hymn Book*) **Take my gifts** (*Go Before Us*) **Through all the changing scenes of life** (*Hymns Old and New: New Anglican Edition*) **Your love, O God, has called us here** (*Hymns of Glory, Songs of Praise*)
Suggested Music	**May love be ours** CD: *Holy Gifts*, Stephen Dean, OCP Publications OR The couple can choose some music for the end of the service – maybe music they had at their wedding. OR The organist can play a wedding march.
Action	Decorate two candles with the names of couple. (See 'How to Put a Design on to a Candle' on page 131.) These can be lit and placed on the altar. Decorate a candle with the words of a blessing and give the candle to the couple at the end of the service. (See 'How to Put a Design on to a Candle' on page 131, or print sticky labels to stick on the candles.)

Fill the church with balloons or flowers the colour of the anniversary being celebrated: 25 years is silver, 30 years is pearl, 40 years is ruby, 50 years is gold, 55 years is emerald, 60 years is diamond, 65 years is sapphire, 70 years is platinum.

It is traditional in some mainland European countries for the bride and groom to give their wedding guests sugared almonds at their wedding. Small packs of these or suitable sweets can be given to the congregation at the end of the service.

Small foil-wrapped heart-shaped chocolates can be stuck on to cards. The cards can have two pictures on them, one of the couple on their wedding day, the other a more recent picture of them. Suitable words can be put on the cards. Everyone can be given a card after the service.

Make an altar frontal or banners to hang in church reflecting the words about love from 1 Corinthians 13.1–13. (See 'How to Make a Paper Altar Frontal' on page 117 and template of 'Love is' design on page 116. See 'How to Make and Hang Banners' on page 113, and template of 'Love Always …' design on page 115.)

Make heart-shaped biscuits to serve at the end of the service. (See 'How to Make Heart-Shaped Biscuits' on page 147.)

ORDER FOR PRAYER AND DEDICATION AFTER A CIVIL MARRIAGE

Introduction

The Welcome
Preface
Prayers of Penitence
The Collect
Readings
Sermon

The Dedication

Prayers
The Blessing

PRAYER AND DEDICATION AFTER A CIVIL MARRIAGE

Many couples today get married in a civil ceremony and afterwards decide they would also like to have their marriage blessed in church. It may well be that they have decided to have a civil ceremony because one or both of them are divorced. In this service there is an acknowledging of things that have gone wrong in the past and a turning to a future full of new hope and expectation. Children of one or both of the married couple might be welcomed as part of the celebration.

The Welcome	The Lord be with you. **And also with you.**

Today we welcome N and N to this church as man and wife.

They have declared their love and made their marriage vows in [*place*] and now stand before God and in the presence of their families and friends, and this congregation, to ask for God's blessing on their new marriage, declaring to all here that they welcome God's love into their lives together.

Let us remain silent for a moment, stilling our thoughts, and bringing N and N to our hearts and minds.

This is the day the Lord has made.

Let us rejoice and be glad in it!

Bible Readings   **Two are better than one**

Two are better than one, because they have a good reward for their toil. For if they fall, one will lift up the other; but woe to one who is alone and falls and does not have another to help.

Again, if two lie together, they keep warm; but how can one keep warm alone? And though one might prevail against another, two will withstand one. A threefold cord is not quickly broken.

Ecclesiastes 4.9–12

The wedding at Cana

On the third day there was a wedding in Cana of Galilee, and the mother of Jesus was there. Jesus and his disciples had also been invited to the wedding. When the wine gave out, the mother of Jesus said to him, 'They have no wine.' And Jesus said to her, 'Woman, what concern is that to you and to me? My hour has not yet come.' His mother said to the servants, 'Do whatever he tells you.' Now standing there were six stone water-jars for the Jewish rites of purification, each holding twenty or thirty gallons. Jesus said to them, 'Fill the jars with water.' And they filled them up to the brim. He said to them, 'Now draw some out, and take it to the chief steward.' So they took it. When the steward tasted the water that had become wine, and did not know where it came from (though the servants who had drawn the water knew), the steward called the bridegroom and said to him, 'Everyone serves the good wine first, and then the inferior wine after the guests have become drunk. But you have kept the good wine until now.' Jesus did this, the first of his signs, in Cana of Galilee, and revealed his glory; and his disciples believed in him.

John 2.1–11

Other Readings   **This day I married my best friend**
Author unknown

This day I married my best friend:

the one I laugh with as we share life's wondrous zest,
as we find new enjoyments and experience all that's best

the one I live for because the world seems brighter
as our happy times are better and our burdens feel much lighter

the one I love with every fibre of my soul.
We used to feel vaguely incomplete, now together we are whole.

Rite of Welcome for Children

N and N have declared their love for each other and are beginning their new life as a married couple. Their lives have a new shape and a new pattern. Their children's lives, too, will be woven into this new shape and pattern, and we are now going to ask N and N to welcome each other and their child/children into their new family.

The couple and their children come forward. The mother and father are each given a candle which they light from the Paschal Candle

The mother, on her behalf and on her children's behalf, says to the father and his children

We welcome you into our family.
As we begin this new adventure together may we learn to share our joys and sorrows, and be gentle, patient and loving with each other.

The father, on his behalf and on his children's behalf, repeats these words to the mother and her children

The mother and father then move to the altar and light the single candle together saying

May the light of Christ shine in our lives
and our children's lives
as we begin this new life together as one family.

The congregation respond

May the light of Christ shine on this new family.
Thanks be to God!

Thanksgiving Prayers

God of forgiveness, we thank you that you always allow everyone to say 'Sorry' and start anew.
Thank you, Lord.

God of joy, we thank you for the wonder of happiness and celebration.
Thank you, Lord.

God of community, we thank you for loved ones, families and friends, and for the way in which two can come together to support and love one another.
Thank you, Lord.

God of peace, we thank you for your stillness and blessing that comes when rejoicing and celebration are over and a new journey is beginning.
Thank you, Lord.

The couple   God of love, forgiveness, joy, community and peace, we thank you for the myriad of blessings being showered upon us today. We pray these blessings will be for ever with us as we go forward together, today and every day to come.
Amen

The Blessing   May God the Father protect you.
May God the Son guide your path.
May God the Holy Spirit fill you with all joy.
May the Holy Trinity bless and keep you.
Today and always.
Amen

Suggested Hymns and Songs   **Brother, sister, let me serve you**
(*Hymns of Glory, Songs of Praise*)

I will be beside you
(*This book*, p. 30)

Jesus put this song into our hearts
(*Songs of Fellowship*)

Let there be love shared among us
(*Complete Anglican Hymns Old and New*)

Love changes everything
(*Sheet music from The Really Useful Company*)

Your love, O God, has called us here
(*Hymns of Glory, Songs of Praise*)

Action

A candle each for the bride and groom and a chunky candle with the words 'See, I am making all things new' written on it (see 'How to Put a Design on to a Candle' on page 131). Place the chunky candle on the altar at the beginning of the service.

The couple may like to choose the flowers to decorate the church.

After the service offer celebration coffee and cake to everyone present.

Display photographs from the civil wedding on a board.

PRAYER AND DEDICATION AFTER A CIVIL MARRIAGE OVERSEAS

Marriage overseas is becoming increasingly popular. This might be for many reasons, not least the (hopeful) guarantee of a hot, sunny day. It might be that the couple want a small celebration in a romantic location where they can then spend their honeymoon rather than having to organize a traditional church wedding and reception at home, with all that that entails. Or maybe the couple are working and living overseas and there are real logistical reasons why they want to be married in a civil ceremony where they are living at the time. After the couple return home they may well decide that they would like their marriage blessed in their local church with family and friends and the church congregation.

The Welcome	The Lord be with you. **And also with you.**
	Today we welcome N and N to this church as man and wife. They have declared their love and made their marriage vows in [*place*] and now stand before God and in the presence of their families and friends in this holy place to ask for God's blessing on their marriage and to dedicate their lives to him.
	Let us remain silent for a moment, stilling our thoughts, and bringing N and N to our hearts and minds.
Bible Readings	**Clothe yourselves with love and let peace rule in your hearts**
	As God's chosen ones, holy and beloved, clothe yourselves with compassion, kindness, humility, meekness, and patience. Bear

with one another and, if anyone has a complaint against another, forgive each other; just as the Lord has forgiven you, so you also must forgive. Above all, clothe yourselves with love, which binds everything together in perfect harmony. And let the peace of Christ rule in your hearts, to which indeed you were called in the one body. And be thankful. Let the word of Christ dwell in you richly; teach and admonish one another in all wisdom; and with gratitude in your hearts sing psalms, hymns, and spiritual songs to God. And whatever you do, in word or deed, do everything in the name of the Lord Jesus, giving thanks to God the Father through him.

Colossians 3.12–17

The Beatitudes

When Jesus saw the crowds, he went up the mountain; and after he sat down, his disciples came to him. Then he began to speak, and taught them, saying:
   'Blessed are the poor in spirit, for theirs is the kingdom of heaven.
   'Blessed are those who mourn, for they will be comforted.
   'Blessed are the meek, for they will inherit the earth.
   'Blessed are those who hunger and thirst for righteousness, for they will be filled.
   'Blessed are the merciful, for they will receive mercy.
   'Blessed are the pure in heart, for they will see God.
   'Blessed are the peacemakers, for they will be called children of God.
   'Blessed are those who are persecuted for righteousness' sake, for theirs is the kingdom of heaven.'

Matthew 5.1–10

Other Reading

Two doves
Author Unknown

Two doves meeting in the sky
Two loves hand in hand eye to eye
Two parts of a loving whole
Two hearts and a single soul.

Two stars shining big and bright
Two fires bringing warmth and light
Two songs played in perfect tune
Two flowers growing into bloom.

Two doves gliding in the air
Two loves free without a care
Two parts of a loving whole
Two hearts and a single soul.

Prayers
Using Psalm 67

**God be gracious to us and bless us
and make his face to shine upon us.**

We pray today for N and N as they stand before you.
May their lives be blessed with good health and joy.
May they know your presence with them in all things,
**That your way may be known upon earth,
your saving power among all nations.**

We pray that the marriage of N and N will be filled with love.
We pray that their love for one another will mirror
the love you have for all people.
We pray that they will grow in faith, live in your truth and
walk in your way.
**God be gracious to us and bless us
and make his face to shine upon us.**

We pray for ourselves, our loved ones and our friends.
May we be worthy of your blessing and grace.
May we reflect your shining light in our lives.
**O let the nations rejoice and be glad,
for you will judge the peoples righteously
and govern the nations upon earth.**

We pray for the peace of your wounded world.
May we all become peacemakers for those around us.
May the leaders of all the nations learn to speak gentle words
of peace and reconciliation to each other,
so that your world may be healed.

**God be gracious to us and bless us
and make his face to shine upon us.**

We pray for those who suffer in body, mind or spirit.
May they know your healing touch in the midst of their pain.
May we reach out to those in distress and bring comfort.
**Then shall the earth bring forth her increase,
and God, our own God, will bless us.**

We pray for this day and all that tomorrow holds.
We pray for N and N as they begin their journey together.
May they be blessed with children and a home,
where all are nurtured and made welcome.
**God will bless us,
and all the ends of the earth shall fear him.
Amen**

The Blessing

May God the Father bless and watch over you.
May God the Son walk by your side.
May God the Holy Spirit fill you with peace
now and always.
Amen

Suggested Hymns and Songs

As man and woman we were made
(*Songs of God's People*)

Like the murmur of a dove's song
(*Hymns of Glory, Songs of Praise*)

Lord of all loving
(*Laudate*)

May the grace of Christ our Saviour
(*Hymns Old and New: One Church, One Faith, One Lord*)

She sits like a bird, brooding on the waters
(*Hymns of Glory, Songs of Praise*)

Surprised by joy
(*Laudate*)

Suggested Music   **Dominus Spiritus est**
CD: *Christe Lux Mundi*, Taizé Community

Spirit Divine
CD: *Sacred Dance*, Keith Duke, Kevin Mayhew

The Road to Home
CD: *Celtic Roots & Rhythms – Homecoming*, Nick and Anita Haigh, ICC

Action   The couple may like to choose the flowers to decorate the church.

If *Two Doves* is being read, make a stole and altar frontal illustrated with doves. (See 'How to Make a Stole' on page 121 and template of 'Doves and Leaves' design on page 126. See 'How to Make a Paper Altar Frontal' on page 117 and templates of 'Two Doves' designs on page 127.)

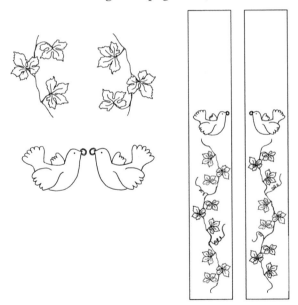

After the service offer celebration coffee and cake to everyone present.

Display photographs from the overseas wedding on a board.

PART FOUR: WELCOME BACK TO CHURCH AFTER A HONEYMOON

WELCOME BACK TO CHURCH AFTER A HONEYMOON

Here are words which might be used during a service to welcome a couple back to church after their honeymoon. Often members of the congregation may not have been at the couple's wedding, or the wedding may have taken place in a different location. Including a welcome during a service, where the couple are present, gives the church family a chance to acknowledge the marriage and offer their good wishes, love and support. The welcome might happen during, or at the end of, a regular Sunday service. Where it is placed and when it should happen needs to be decided by the minister and the couple together.

The couple might like to choose one of the hymns to be sung in the service, possibly one that they had at their wedding.

The minister explains that N and N have recently married and that the congregation are going to welcome them back from their honeymoon.

The couple are invited to come up to the front of the church

The Welcome   This is the day the Lord has made!
Let us rejoice and be glad in it!

Lord, we thank you that N and N were married *xx* weeks ago. At their wedding service they exchanged solemn vows and exchanged rings to symbolize their marriage. May we, the church family in this place, support them as they journey onwards together. We welcome them into this family as a married couple, and we rejoice with them at this time.
Do you all agree to support N and N in their marriage?
We do.

The couple are then given an empty 'Bag for Life'. (See 'How to Make a "Bag for Life"' on page 136 for instructions on how to make the bag, and 'How to Put a Design on to a Candle' on page 131.) The items to go into the bag are given to them one at a time. This can be done by different members of the congregation. The bag can have a label which lists the contents. (See label designs on page 137.)

Minister	We offer you this bag to help you carry all you will need for your journey together.
Voice One	We give you a candle to light your path.
Voice Two	We give you a Bible to guide you along the way.
Voice Three	We give you some party-poppers to help you have fun and celebrate the joy of life.
Voice Four	We give you a bottle of water to quench your thirst and give you life in abundance.
Voice Five	We give you some bulbs to plant to help you live a life of hope and expectation.
Voice Six	We give you some chocolate to break and share.
All together	**We give you our love and support today.**
Minister	*N* and *N* May the God of love bless you, may the friendship of Christ walk beside you, may the joy and excitement of the Holy Spirit never leave you, may your path be smooth, may your journey be blessed, may you skip along together until your lives' end. **Amen**

BAG
FOR
LIFE

PART FIVE: HEALING PRAYERS IN CHURCH AT THE ENDING OF A MARRIAGE

HEALING PRAYERS IN CHURCH AT THE ENDING OF A MARRIAGE

Here is a short liturgy for healing prayer in church following a divorce. It provides an opportunity for the divorced person to come to church and, in the company of a small group of family and friends, offer *her/his* sadness and feelings of failure, or hurt, to God. It is a time to let go of the past, and of what might have been, in the sure knowledge of God's compassion. It is appropriate that the church community should reach out in pastoral love and support at a time when the divorced person is feeling most lost and vulnerable.

Prayers   Lord, we believe that when two or three people gather together you are with them.
We ask you to be here with us now.

A candle is lit

Lord, we know that you chose to be with the wounded and the broken-hearted.
We ask you today to come near to N as *she/he* offers you *her/his* sorrow and despair at the breakdown and ending of *her/his* marriage.

Lord, we know that in your mercy you bring healing and solace.
We ask you to soothe the pain that N is feeling and make *her/him* whole again.

Lord, we know, too, that you forgive us when we fail.
We make mistakes over and over again, yet still you love us.
We ask for your compassion as N acknowledges all that led to
the failure of *her/his* marriage and breaking of *her/his* marriage
vows, and asks your forgiveness.

Those present now hold N silently in prayer as she/he offers to God, either
aloud or silently, those things for which she/he is sorry or for which she/he seeks
forgiveness

As those present remain silent N may remove her/his wedding ring and place it
beside the lit candle – the light of Christ – a light which can overcome all darkness.
N's pain, and the wedding ring around which the pain is focused, is now handed
over to the safe keeping of Christ. As there were supporters who witnessed the
placing of the ring on N's finger at her/his marriage service, so now there are sup-
porters who witness its removal

Lord, we know that from death comes new life, and that from
endings come new beginnings.
We pray that following the ending of N's marriage there will,
slowly and gently, be new life and a new beginning.

Lord, your love for us is more than we can possibly
comprehend.
We ask you to enfold N in your love so that, even when *she/*
***he* feels empty and sorrowful, *she/he* will know that you are**
there.

Lord, in this church, where your people meet to celebrate their
joy, and to acknowledge their sorrow, we pray that N will find
comfort and companionship.
As the people of God in this holy place, we offer N love and
support in your name, and promise to walk with *her/him* as
***she/he* begins to rebuild *her/his* life.**

Lord, we come to you,
hear the cry of our hearts.
Meet N in *her/his* brokenness,
heal *her/his* pain,

forgive *her/his* failure to keep *her/his* vows,
and surround *her/him* with your love
that, putting *her/his* trust in you,
she/he may put this sorrow behind *her/him*
and begin to look forward and live again.
Amen

The candle is snuffed

Additional Resources

Reflection   **Luke 15.4–7 The Message**
                       Eugene H. Peterson

Suppose one of you had a hundred sheep and lost one. Wouldn't
you leave the ninety-nine in the wilderness and go after the lost
one until you found it? When found, you can be sure you would
put it across your shoulders, rejoicing, and when you got home
call in your friends and neighbours, saying, 'Celebrate with
me! I've found my lost sheep!' Count on it – there's more joy
in heaven over one sinner's rescued life than over ninety-nine
good people in no need of rescue.

Father, I have been wandering in the wilderness of unhappy
marriage and break-up. The path has been very rough, and
very painful. I have lost my way. Now it is over and '*I am divorced*'. That sounds so hard and difficult to say and accept.
I didn't want it to be like this. I need to be found by you and
brought home. Carry me for a while. Forgive me – we got it all
wrong. Help me home into your loving, forgiving arms, to rest
for a while and heal.
Amen

Song during a time of grief

Lord, we pray be near us

1 Lord, we pray, be near us,
   In this time of grief;
   Bring us peace and healing,
   Solace and relief:
   Heaviness surrounds us
   Like a storm-filled cloud;
   Sounds of day and sunlight
   Now seem harsh and loud.

2 As the shadows deepen
   Chasing out the light;
   Hold us in your hand, and
   Lead us through the night:
   May we, in our sorrow,
   Feel your loving care;
   When life overwhelms us
   Know that you are near.

3 In the end we trust that
   All shall be made well;
   Send your Holy Spirit
   In our hearts to dwell:
   Gently, oh so gently,
   Day must dawn again;
   Shafts of golden sunlight
   Shining through the rain.

Text © Jan Brind 2004
Music © David Davies 2006
This song can also be sung to Cranham 65 65D

OR

The Lord's my shepherd
(*Hymns Old and New: New Anglican Edition*)

Song during a time of grief

Jan Brind

David Davies

Lord we pray be near us in this time of grief; bring us peace and heal - ing, so-lace and re-

lief: hea - vi - ness sur - rounds us like a storm-filled cloud;

sounds of day and sun - light now seem harsh and loud.

PART SIX: HOW TO MAKE

HOW TO MAKE BANNERS AND ALTAR FRONTALS

Wedding banners and altar frontals can add much to a church wedding. When considering making banners and/or an altar frontal, decide if these are to be for one particular wedding or whether the church might be able to use them again. If they are to be used for just one wedding, they can be made to match a couple's colour scheme and even mention the couple's names and reflect something of their lives and the journey they are about to start together. If the banners and altar frontal are to be used again in the church for other weddings, think about using words from the wedding service or a more general wedding design and theme.

Banners and altar frontals can be made from paper or material. Window blind fabric works well. It hangs well, is easy to cut, and doesn't tear.

Here are some of the words and phrases from the wedding liturgy that might be used in a design:

The Lord bless you and watch over you.
  The Lord make his face shine upon you,
    and give you peace.

Love always
  trusts, hopes, perseveres.
Love never
  fails.

Love is patient and kind,
  does not envy or boast,
    is not proud or rude.

Love one another.

Fill them with your love.

Abide in my love that your joy may be complete.

Be patient,
   bear with one another.

Rejoice in the Lord always!

May the God of hope
   fill you with joy and peace.

Companions in joy,
   comforters in sorrow,
     strength in need.

God is love,
   and those who live in love live in God
     and God lives in them.

HOW TO MAKE AND HANG BANNERS

Decorate the church or reception venue with banners!

Bunting banners

You will need a supply of A4 paper.

1 Put one letter on each piece of paper. The letters can be printed from a computer using WordArt. Position the letter on the paper so there is room for a 2-inch (5 cm) fold at the top of each sheet of paper.
2 Make a 2-inch (5 cm) fold at the top of each sheet of paper.
3 Place a piece of string along the fold and staple the folds down. Make sure not to catch the string in the staples so as to allow the pieces of paper to be slid along the string.
4 Decorate the letters with hearts, spots, stars, etc. Keep the decorations inside the letters. This is a lovely exercise for children to do. Leave a blank piece of paper between words. You might put the couple's names and the date on the bunting, or a Bible quote from the wedding service.

Large banners

Decide how big your banners are going to be. A roll of lining paper can be cut to size. To decorate the banners see 'How to put a design on an altar frontal'.

The easiest way to hang a large banner is to make a 'tunnel' along the top by folding over the paper or material and fixing in place. To hang the banner up, put a pole through the tunnel. Then either hook up both ends of the pole or attach string/ribbon/cord to either end of the pole and suspend it from a central hook. If there are pillars in the church, the banners can be fixed or hung from these.

HOW TO MAKE BUNTING BANNERS

1

2

3

4

A DESIGN FOR A BANNER

LOVE
ALWAYS...
TRUSTS
HOPES
PERSEVERES
LOVE
NEVER...
FAILS

LOVE IS patient & kind

DOES NOT envy or boast

IS NOT proud or rude

HOW TO MAKE A PAPER ALTAR FRONTAL

1 Take a roll of wallpaper – either lining paper or the reverse side of a patterned paper, the thicker the better. Do not use an embossed paper as nothing will stick to it.

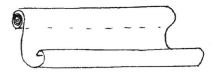

2 Measure the width of the altar and roll out the paper to match. You will need to cut two lengths to make up the height.

3 Stick the middle join together with glue and adjust the height at the middle by overlapping the two sheets of paper. Do not try to cut the paper at the bottom or top, as it is very difficult to cut a straight line. Be careful not to let the glue get on to the front.

4 Turn the paper over so the back is uppermost. Stick brown parcel tape along all the edges and across the middle join – this will stop the edges tearing and strengthen the paper when it is fixed to the altar.

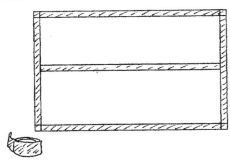

5 Think about how you are going to fix the altar frontal to the altar before you put the design on.

6 Now all you have to do is decorate the front.

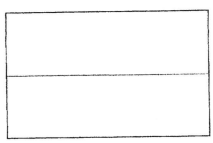

HOW TO USE THE NAMES OF THE COUPLE GETTING MARRIED ON BANNERS OR ALTAR FRONTALS

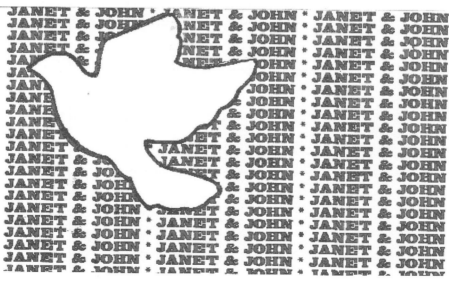

HOW TO PUT A DESIGN ON AN ALTAR FRONTAL

1 Decide what you want to say on the altar frontal. You might use words such as 'Love is patient and kind, does not envy or boast, is not proud or rude.'
2 Think about the background. Will it be plain, or do you need to put a design on it before putting on the words?
3 Write the words on a computer using a program such as WordArt.
4 Remember that the words have to fit the space, so choose the font size carefully and think about the shape the words will make and therefore how they will be placed on the frontal.
5 Decide how you will put the words on the frontal.

    a **Spray over the letters**. Cut out the letters and place them on the background, sticking them lightly with glue so they don't move when sprayed over. Spray over the letters. Carefully remove the letters, and the shapes of the letters will be left on the background.

b **Make a stencil and spray through the stencil**. Mark the letters on a large piece of paper in the shape you want them to be on the altar frontal. Carefully cut out the shapes of the letters using a craft knife. Put a small amount of glue on the back of the stencil to hold it in place. Place the stencil on background. Either spray through the stencil, or, using a stencil brush, paint through the stencil. Remove stencil and the letters will be on the background.

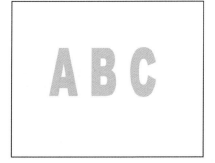

c **Cut out the letters in either paper or fabric and stick them on to the background**. Carefully mark where the letters will go before sticking them on. The letters should be made in a contrasting colour to the background so that they stand out well.

HOW TO MAKE A STOLE

There are many shapes for stoles. They can vary in length and width and in the shape around the neck. For this purpose the shape will be kept as simple as possible, with the neck being shaped to fit the person the stole is being made for.

1 Decide on the width for the stole. About 4½ inches (12cm) would be a common width.

2 Cut out four pieces of fabric 6½ inches (17cm) wide. The length of the stole will depend on the height of the person who is going to wear it. It usually falls to about mid-shin on the person. The length will also be governed by how broad-shouldered the person is, so it may well be helpful to measure the person before cutting out the fabric.

3 Pieces 1 and 2 are for the front, 3 and 4 are for the back.

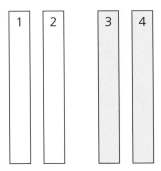

4 With right sides facing, place pieces 1 and 2 on top of each other. Pin and sew the neck as shown in the diagram. It would be good at this stage to fit the neck on the person the stole is being made for.

5 Repeat the same exercise with pieces 3 and 4.

6 Put the design onto the front pieces.

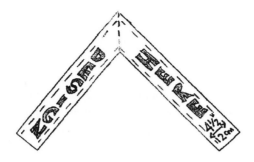

7 With right sides facing place pieces 1 and 2 on to pieces 3 and 4 and pin them together, making sure that the neck joins are placed together.

8 Sew up the sides of the pieces, making a long tube.

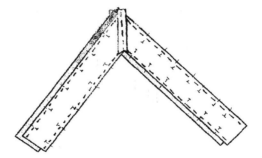

9 Turn the 'tube' inside out.

10 Press the edges with an iron.

11 Turn up the ends and stitch by hand.

A PATCHWORK WEDDING STOLE OR BANNER

Each patchwork letter can be made by the family and friends of the bride and groom, and then be put together as a stole or banner for the service. The words used can be chosen to fit the service

A PATCHWORK BANNER

A CANDLE STOLE

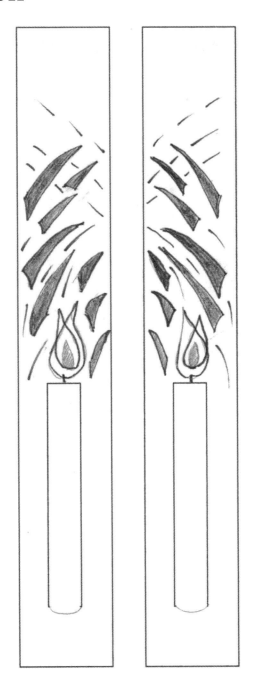

DOVES AND LEAVES STOLE

LEAVES AND DOVES

HOW TO PUT A DESIGN ON TO FABRIC USING APPLIQUÉ

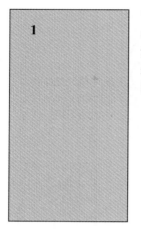

1 Measure and cut out the background fabric. If needed, stiffen fabric with iron-on stiffener.

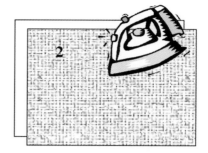

2 Choose the fabric to be sewn on to the background. Iron a piece of stiffener on to the back of the fabric.

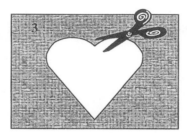

3 Place the shape to be used on to the stiffener and cut the shape out.

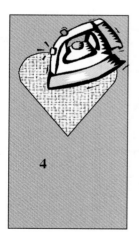

4 Place a piece of 'wonderweb' between the cut-out shape and the background and iron on. This keeps the shape in position when it is being sewn on to the background.

5 Sew the shape on to the background.

A STOLE – DECORATED WITH THE WORDS 'FILL THEM WITH YOUR LOVE'

This is a wonderful celebration stole. The simple words are taken from a prayer in the marriage service in The Alternative Service Book 1980 – Additional Prayers.

> Almighty God, our heavenly Father,
> who gave marriage to be a source of
> blessing to mankind,
> we thank you for the joys of family life.
> May we know your presence and peace
> in our homes;
> ***fill them with your love,***
> and use them for your glory;
> through Jesus Christ our Lord. Amen

The two Os in *Love* and *Your* are joined together.
Make wonderful 'whooshes' going from one side of the stole to the other.
If there is any significant fabric belonging to the bride or groom add it to the stole.
A piece of fabric from the bride's or bridesmaids' dresses works well.

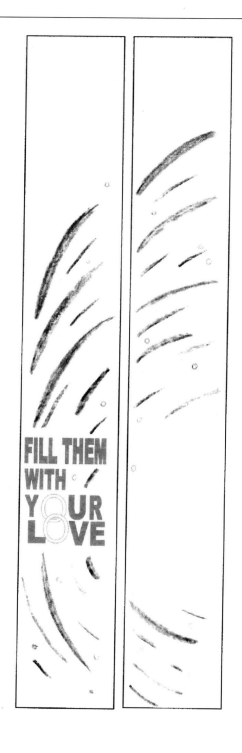

HOW TO PUT A DESIGN ON TO A CANDLE

Putting a design on to a candle is simple, but may need a little practice. Working on a rounded surface can be quite difficult the first time it is tried. Square candles are easier to work on. The bigger the candle, the easier it is to put on the design – very thin ones have little surface to work on.

1 First buy the candle, bearing in mind where it is to go and what the design is to be.
2 Decide on the colours to be used.
3 Work out the design to go on the candle, keeping it very simple.
4 Wrap a piece of paper round the candle to see how big the design should be and how it will be positioned on the candle. Most candles will only be seen from one side, so remember to design the candle with that in mind.
5 Now draw the design on the same piece of paper with a strong line. (If drawing is too difficult, use a computer to type and print off words in a big, bold font.)
6 Put clear adhesive tape on to the top and bottom of the design paper and stick in place on the candle.
7 With a pen or pencil go over the design and gently press the design into the candle surface.
8 Take the paper off the candle and the design should be visible on the surface.
9 With a waterproof felt pen, fill in the design.
10 Using relief outliner made to use on glass, go round the outline of the design.
11 Leave to dry.

Decorating a candle using shapes cut from wax sheets

Thin coloured sheets of wax can be bought from an art and craft supplier such as Opitec (www.opitec.co.uk). Cut shapes out of the wax to decorate a candle. Use our dove shapes, or draw your own, and follow the directions above for transferring the shapes on to the candle, or use shaped metal or plastic biscuit or pastry cutters, easily found in cook shops that supply cake decoration materials. This is a wonderful way to add an extra design to a candle. Opitec can also supply pre-cut doves and wedding rings.

How to put a design on to a candle

WORDS TO GO ON TO A CANDLE BEING HANDED FROM THE PARENTS TO THEIR CHILD

WORDS TO GO ON A CHUNKY CANDLE TO GO ON THE ALTAR

DECORATING CANDLES WITH RIBBON AND FLOWERS

DOVE SHAPES TO CUT OUT AND PUT ON TO CANDLES

HOW TO MAKE A 'BAG FOR LIFE'

1 Cut out one rectangular piece of plain fabric about 33 inches (84 cm) × 16 inches (41 cm) for the body of the bag (A).

2 Cut out one piece of fabric about 106 inches (270 cm) × 5 inches (12 cm) for the handle (B). If necessary this can be made up of pieces of fabric sewed together.

3 Take the large piece of fabric (A) and fold over and sew the two short ends. Iron flat.

4 Take the long piece of fabric (B). Fold over about ½ inch (1 cm) along one long edge and iron flat. Then fold over the other long edge to tuck under the first folded edge. Sew down the centre to catch both the edges. Iron the bag handle flat.

5 Lay the handle along the right side of the bag as shown, starting and finishing at the centre fold of the bag. Pin in place, making a complete circle, and then sew the handle on to the bag.

6 Write **BAG FOR LIFE** on the bag.

7 Turn the bag right sides together and sew down the two side edges.

8 Turn the bag round the right way and press the edges.

9 The bag is now ready to be filled.

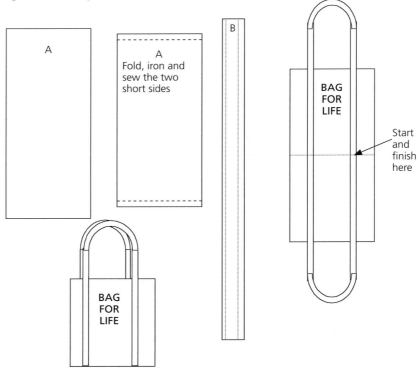

LABEL FOR A BAG FOR LIFE WHEN READING THE BANNS

- **A candle** - to light the way
- **A Prayer Card** – a reminder that God is ever present
- **Bath bubbles** – to relax in
- **Aromatherapy oil** - to soothe frayed nerves
- **A comedy DVD** – to share laughter
- **Fizzy water** - to refresh and revitalise
- **Chocolate** - to break and share
- **Wine** – to break open in case of emergency

LABEL FOR A BAG FOR LIFE WHEN WELCOMING A COUPLE BACK FROM THEIR HONEYMOON

- We give you a **candle** – to light your path
- We give you a **Bible** – to guide you along the way
- We give you some **party poppers** – to help you have fun and celebrate the joy of life
- We give you a **bottle of water** – to quench your thirst and give you life in abundance
- We give you some **bulbs** – to plant to help you live a life of hope and expectation
- We give you some **chocolate** – to break and share

HOW TO MAKE A DRAWSTRING BAG FOR CHILDREN

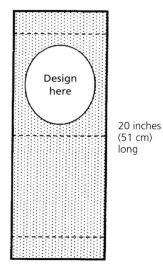

20 inches
(51 cm)
long

12 inches
(30 cm) wide

1 Cut out a piece of fabric about 20 inches (51 cm) long and 12 inches (30 cm) wide.

2 If you are going to put a design on the bag, do it now. The names of the couple and the date might be added.

3 Make a channel to take the string. Fold the fabric over about 2 inches (5 cm), on both of the short sides, iron it flat and sew along the bottom to make a channel.

4 With the right sides facing, fold the fabric in half in the centre, bringing the two short ends together.

5 Sew up the sides of the bag.

6 Turn the bag round the right way and press the seams flat.

7 Thread the string or cord through the two channels and tie the ends together.

8 Before the service fill the bag with small soft toys and books.

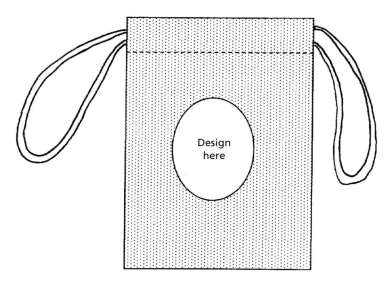

HOW TO MAKE AN APRON

1 Take a rectangular piece of fabric.
2 Fold over and press all the edges.
3 Sew down the edges.
4 Decide which is the top.

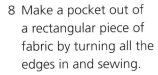

5 Fold the apron in half, lengthways, and mark the centre.

6 Unfold again and fold over the two top corners about one-third towards the centre and about one-third down the long sides.

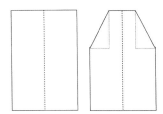

7 Press the folds and sew.

8 Make a pocket out of a rectangular piece of fabric by turning all the edges in and sewing.

9 Put design either onto the pocket or onto the apron and the pocket.

10 Sew pocket on front of apron leaving the top open.

11 Sew on a neck loop and tapes to tie the apron – these could be made from the same fabric or from white tape.

your design here

YOUR
DESIGN
HERE

RENEWAL OF MARRIAGE VOWS FOR MORE THAN ONE COUPLE CARDS ONE AND TWO

Card to be read by couple when renewing marriage vows

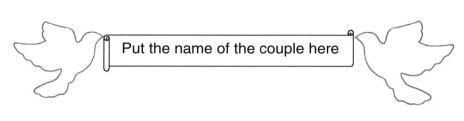

Put the name of the couple here

MAY THE LIGHT OF CHRIST SHINE ON US
AS WE NOW MAKE OUR VOWS,
AND MAY WE REFLECT THIS LIGHT
AS WE GO FROM THIS PLACE TO
CONTINUE OUR MARRIAGE TOGETHER.

MAY THE LIGHT OF CHRIST
SHINE ON US AS WE NOW
MAKE OUR VOWS, AND
MAY WE REFLECT THIS
LIGHT AS WE GO FROM
THIS PLACE TO CONTINUE
OUR MARRIAGE TOGETHER.

PEW CARD DESIGNS ONE AND TWO

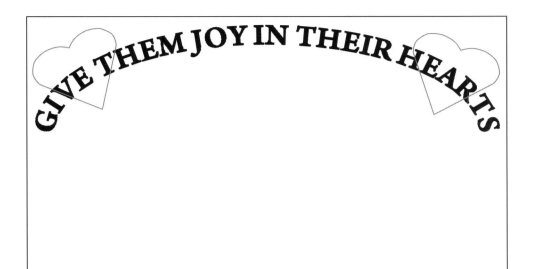

PEW CARD DESIGNS THREE AND FOUR

YOU ARE HUSBAND & WIFE

praise God !

PEW CARD DESIGNS FIVE AND SIX

sing alleluia

to the Lord!

God bless you both!

BLESSING CARD

ANNIVERSARY CARDS ONE AND TWO

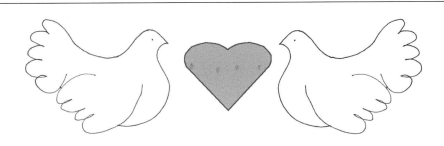

NAMES HERE
WISHING YOU EVERY BLESSING
ON YOUR
FIRST WEDDING ANNIVERSARY
FROM ALL AT ST N CHURCH

wishing you every blessing
on your wedding anniversary

CARDS TO TAKE HOME

THE LORD BLESS YOU ON YOUR WEDDING DAY

Name of couple here

Date and place of wedding here

THE LORD BLESS YOU & KEEP YOU & GIVE YOU PEACE

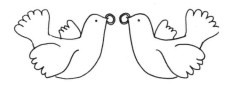

Name of couple here

Date and place of wedding here

HOW TO MAKE HEART-SHAPED BISCUITS

You will need:
    Heart-shaped biscuit cutters.
    Clear cellophane.
    Coloured ribbon.

Oven temperature 350°F (180°C) Gas Mark 4.

Ingredients:
    100 g (4 oz) soft butter or margarine.
    100 g (4 oz) caster sugar.
    1 egg, beaten.
    200 g (8 oz) flour.
    (Icing sugar and pink food colouring for glacé icing)

Method:
Grease two baking trays. Cream the butter and sugar until pale and fluffy. Add the egg a little at a time, beating after each addition. Stir in the flour and mix to a fairly firm dough. Knead lightly and roll out 0.5 cm (¼ inch) thick on a floured board. Carefully cut heart shapes with the biscuit cutter. Lift on to a greased tray and bake in the top of the oven for 15–20 minutes until firm and very lightly browned. Leave on the trays to cool for a few minutes before transferring to wire racks. Ice the biscuits with pink glacé icing and decorate some of them with 'hundreds and thousands'.

Place two or three biscuits in a cellophane 'bag' and tie it up with ribbon. The bags can be placed in a basket and handed out by children.

This recipe makes about 20 biscuits.

HOW TO MAKE SIMPLE CHOCOLATE FUDGE

You will need:
    Clear cellophane.
    Coloured ribbon.

Ingredients:
    500 g (1lb 2oz) dark chocolate.
    75 g (2¾ oz) soft unsalted butter.
    400 g (14 oz) condensed milk.
    ½ teaspoon vanilla extract.

Method:
Grease a 20 cm (8 inch) square cake tin. Break the chocolate into small pieces and with the butter and condensed milk either microwave in a bowl until just melted, or melt in a saucepan. Do not allow to boil. Mix in the vanilla extract and beat until the mixture is thickened. Place mixture in the cake tin and chill until firm. Turn the fudge out and cut into squares.
Place three or four pieces in a cellophane 'bag' and tie it up with ribbon. The bags can be placed in a basket and handed out by children.

This recipe makes about 25 pieces.

Variations:

To make chocolate mocha fudge omit the vanilla essence and add 1 tablespoon of strong coffee mixed with 1 teaspoon hot water.

To make chocolate nut fudge add 60 g (2 oz) chopped walnuts to the mixture with the vanilla extract.

PART SEVEN: RESOURCES FOR CREATING SERVICES

A SELECTION OF READINGS AND BLESSINGS

Authors are given where known.

A Celtic blessing

Author unknown

May the road rise to meet you,
May the wind be always at your back.
May the sun shine warm upon your face,
The rains fall soft upon your fields.
And until we meet again,
May God hold you in the palm of his hand.

May God be with you and bless you;
May you see your children's children.
May you be poor in misfortune,
Rich in blessings,
May you know nothing but happiness
From this day forward.

May the road rise to meet you,
May the wind be always at your back,
May the warm rays of sun fall upon your home,
And may the hand of a friend always be near.

May green be the grass you walk on,
May blue be the skies above you,
May pure be the joys that surround you,
May true be the hearts that love you.

A walled garden

Author unknown

Your marriage should have within it a secret and protected space, open to you alone. Imagine it to be a walled garden, entered by a door to which you only hold the key. Within this garden you will cease to be a mother, father, employee, homemaker or any other of the roles which you fulfil in daily life. Here you can be yourselves, two people who love each other. Here you can concentrate on one another's needs. So take each other's hands and go forth to your garden. The time you spend together is not wasted but invested – invested in your future and nurture of your love.

Eskimo love song

Author unknown

You are my husband, you are my wife
My feet shall run because of you
My feet dance because of you
My heart shall beat because of you
My eyes see because of you
My mind thinks because of you
And I shall love, because of you.

Adapted from *Far from the Madding Crowd*

Thomas Hardy

We are all on our own paths, all on our own journeys.
Sometimes the paths cross, and people arrive at the crossing points at the same time and meet each other.
There are greetings, pleasantries are exchanged, and then they move on.

But then once in a while the pleasantries become more, friendship grows, deeper links are made, hands are joined and love flies.

The friendship has turned into love.

Paths are joined, one path with two people walking it, both going in the same direction, and sharing each other's journeys.

Today N and N are joining their paths.

They will now skip together in harmony and love, sharing joys and sorrows, hopes and fears, strengthening and upholding each other as they walk along side by side.

At home by the fire, whenever I look up, there you will be. And whenever you look up, there I shall be.

From *The Prophet*

Kahlil Gibran

Love has no other desire but to fulfil itself.

But if you love and must needs have desires, let these be your desires:

To melt and be like a running brook that sings its melody to the night.

To know the pain of too much tenderness.

To be wounded by your own understanding of love;

And to bleed willingly and joyfully.

To wake at dawn with a winged heart and give thanks for another day of loving;

To rest at the noon hour and meditate love's ecstasy;

To return home at eventide with gratitude;

And then to sleep with a prayer for the beloved in your heart and a song of praise on your lips.

From *This Sunrise of Wonder*

Michael Mayne

There is the mystery of the relationship between two persons: what the marriage service in the Prayer Book calls 'the mystery of one flesh', a man and a woman who, through growing together by the daily unspoken giving and receiving of love in small ways, find that over the years each has been invaded and shaped by the reality of the other, in a way that does not diminish, but rather enhances, each of them. (pages 17 and 18)

Adapted from *This Sunrise of Wonder*

Michael Mayne

Falling in love *(is a cause for wonder)*, especially when that leads to a deep and lifelong commitment; and to give yourself without reserve to that particular mystery is to trust that you are able to be lifted out of the narrowness of self in the give-and-take of love, and in so transcending yourself become more, not less, what you truly are.
(page 52)

I am Love

Author unknown

Some say I can fly on the wind, yet I haven't any wings. Some have found me floating on the open sea, yet I cannot swim. Some have felt my warmth on cold nights, yet I have no flame. And though you cannot see me, I lay between two lovers at the hearth of fireplaces. I am the twinkle in your child's eyes. I am hidden in the lines of your mother's face. I am your father's shield as he guards your home. And yet … Some say I am stronger than steel, yet I am as fragile as a tear. Some have never searched for me, yet I am around them always. Some say I die with loss, yet I am endless. And though you cannot hear me, I dance on the laughter of children. I am woven into the whispers of passion. I am in the blessings of grandmothers. I embrace the cries of newborn babies. And yet … Some say I am a flower, yet I am also the seed. Some have little faith in me, yet I will always believe in them. Some say I cannot cure the ill, yet I nourish the soul. And though you cannot touch me, I am the gentle hand of the kind. I am the fingertips that caress your cheek at night. I am the hug of a child. I am Love.

I love you this much

Author unknown

I love you this much.
Enough to do anything for you, give my life, my love,
my heart and my soul to you and for you.
Enough to willingly give all of my time, efforts, thoughts, talents, trust and prayers to you.

Enough to want to protect you, care for you, guide you, hold you, comfort you,
listen to you, and cry to you and with you.
Enough to be completely comfortable with you, act silly around you,
never have to hide anything from you, and be myself with you.
I love you enough to share all of my sentiments, dreams, goals, fears, hopes and
worries, my entire life with you.
Enough to want the best for you, to wish for your successes,
and to hope for the fulfilment of all your endeavours.
Enough to keep my promises to you
and pledge my loyalty and faithfulness to you.
Enough to cherish your friendship, adore your personality, respect your values and
see you for who you are.
I love you enough to fight for you,
compromise for you, and sacrifice myself for you if need be.
Enough to miss you incredibly when
we're apart, no matter what length
Enough to believe in our relationship, to stand by it through the worst of times,
to have faith in our strength as a couple, and to never give up on us.
Enough to spend the rest of my life with you,
be there for you when you need or want me,
and never, ever want to leave you or live without you.
I love you this much.

Love is

Tessa Wilkinson

Love is
… to wait with anticipation for the key in the door
… to walk down the street with fingers entwined
… to laugh until the tears pour down your cheeks
… to stand together in awe and wonder when something beautiful is shared
… to journey with a spirit of expectation
… to rise above exhaustion
… to always give that little bit more
… to always forgive and start again
… to know total togetherness and at the same time total freedom
Love flies, love runs, love leaps for joy
Love lights a dark place

Love welcomes
Love transforms
Those who love are richly blessed

May love

Tessa Wilkinson

May love
... surround you both
... hold you on your journey
... be the welcome at your door
... be at the centre of your home and family
... be between you and all whom you meet.
Go well, with love in your hearts
and at the centre of all you do.
And the blessing of God Almighty,
Father, Son and Holy Spirit be upon you both
today and always.
Amen

From *The Prophet*

Kahlil Gibran

On Marriage
Then Almitra spoke again and said, And what of Marriage, master?
And he answered saying:
You were born together, and together you shall be for evermore.
You shall be together when the white wings of death scatter your days.
Aye, you shall be together even in the silent memory of God.
But let there be spaces in your togetherness.
And let the winds of the heavens dance between you.
Love one another, but make not a bond of love:
Let it rather be a moving sea between the shores of your souls.
Fill each other's cup but drink not from one cup.
Give one another of your bread but eat not from the same loaf.
Sing and dance together and be joyous, but let each one of you be alone,

Even as the strings of a lute are alone though they quiver with the same music.
Give your hearts, but not into each other's keeping.
For only the hand of Life can contain your hearts.
And stand together yet not too near together:
For the pillars of the temple stand apart,
And the oak tree and cypress grow not in each other's shadow.

Sonnet 116

William Shakespeare

Let me not to the marriage of true minds
admit impediments. Love is not love
which alters when it alteration finds,
or bends with the remover to remove:
Oh, no! It is an ever-fixed mark.
That looks on tempests and is never shaken;
it is the star to every wandering bark,
whose worth's unknown, although his height be taken.
Love's not Time's fool, though rosy lips and cheeks
within his bending sickle's compass come;
love alters not with his brief hours and weeks,
but bears it out even to the edge of doom.
If this be error and upon me proved,
I never writ, nor no man ever loved.

The blessing of the Apaches

Author unknown

Now you will feel no rain
For each of you will be shelter to the other.
Now you will feel no cold
For each of you will be warmth to the other.
Now there is no more loneliness for you
For each of you will be companion to the other.
Now you are two bodies
But there is only one life before you.

Go now to your dwelling place
To enter into the days of your togetherness
And may your days be good, and long, upon the earth.

The most wonderful of all things

Hugh Walpole Sr

The most wonderful of all things in life, I believe, is the discovery of another human being with whom one's relationship has a growing depth, beauty, and joy as the years increase. This inner progressiveness of love between two human beings is a most marvellous thing; it cannot be found by looking for it or by passionately wishing for it. It is a sort of divine accident, and the most wonderful of all things in life.

The passionate shepherd to his love

Christopher Marlowe

Come live with me, and be my love,
And we will all the pleasures prove
That valleys, groves, hills and fields,
Woods, or steepy mountain yields.

And we will sit upon the rocks,
Seeing the shepherds feed their flocks
By shallow rivers, to whose falls
Melodious birds sing madrigals.

And I will make thee beds of roses,
And a thousand fragrant posies,
A cap of flowers, and a kirtle,
Embroidered all with leaves of myrtle.

A gown made of the finest wool
Which from our pretty lambs we pull,
Fair lined slippers for the cold,
With buckles of the purest gold.

A belt of straw and ivy buds,
With coral clasps and amber studs,
And if these pleasures may thee move,
Come live with me, and be my love.

The shepherds' swains shall dance and sing
For thy delight each May-morning;
If these delights thy mind may move,
Then live with me, and be my love.

This day I married my best friend

Author unknown

This day I married my best friend:

the one I laugh with as we share life's wondrous zest,
as we find new enjoyments and experience all that's best

the one I live for because the world seems brighter
as our happy times are better and our burdens feel much
lighter

the one I love with every fibre of my soul.
We used to feel vaguely incomplete, now together we are
whole.

True love

Author unknown

True love is a sacred flame
That burns eternally,
And none can dim its special glow
Or change its destiny.
True love speaks in tender tones
And hears with gentle ear,
True love gives with open heart

And true love conquers fear.
True love makes no harsh demands
It neither rules nor binds,
And true love holds with gentle hands
The hearts that it entwines.

Two doves

Author unknown

Two doves meeting in the sky
Two loves hand in hand eye to eye
Two parts of a loving whole
Two hearts and a single soul

Two stars shining big and bright
Two fires bringing warmth and light
Two songs played in perfect tune
Two flowers growing into bloom

Two doves gliding in the air
Two loves free without a care
Two parts of a loving whole
Two hearts and a single soul.

Wedding prayer

Robert Louis Stevenson

Lord, behold our family here assembled.
We thank you for this place in which we dwell,
for the love that unites us,
for the peace accorded us this day,
for the hope with which we expect the morrow,
for the health, the work, the food,
and the bright skies that make our lives delightful;
for our friends in all parts of the earth.
Amen.

What is love

Author unknown

Sooner or later we begin to understand that love is more than verses on valentines and romance in the movies. We begin to know that love is here and now, real and true, the most important thing in our lives. For love is the creator of our favourite memories and the foundation of our fondest dreams. Love is a promise that is always kept, a fortune that can never be spent, a seed that can flourish in even the most unlikely of places. And this radiance that never fades, this mysterious and magical joy, is the greatest treasure of all – one known only by those who love.

A SELECTION OF
RESOURCE BOOKS

These might be helpful when planning weddings.

A Wee Worship Book, Wild Goose Worship Group, Wild Goose Publications, 1999.

Alternative Weddings: An essential guide for creating your own ceremony, Jane Ross-Macdonald, Taylor Trade Publishing, 1997.

An Order of Marriage for Christians from Different Churches, The Joint Liturgical Group of Great Britain, Canterbury Press, 1999.

Approaches to Prayer: A resource book for groups and individuals, edited by Henry Morgan, SPCK, 1991.

Bread for the Journey: Reflections for every day of the year, Henri J. M. Nouwen, Darton, Longman & Todd, 1996.

Celebrating our Love: Liturgical resources for preparing and celebrating marriage, Novalis, 2002.

Christian Miscellany, Parminder Summon, Lion, 2004.

Common Worship: Pastoral services (2nd edition), Liturgical Commission, Church House Publishing, 2004.

Crafts for Creative Worship: A resource and activity book for parishes, Jan Brind and Tessa Wilkinson, Canterbury Press, 2004.

Creating Uncommon Worship, Richard Giles, Canterbury Press, 2004.

Creative Ideas for Evening Prayer: For seasons, feasts and special occasions, Jan Brind and Tessa Wilkinson, Canterbury Press, 2005.

Enfolded in Love: Daily readings with Julian of Norwich, Julian of Norwich, Darton, Longman & Todd, 1980.

Growing Together: A guide for couples getting married, Andrew Body, Church House Publishing, 2005.

Growing Together – The Course: A complete marriage preparation programme, Andrew Body, Church House Publishing, 2005.

Holy Ground: Liturgies and worship resources for an engaged spirituality, Neil Paynter and Helen Boothroyd, Wild Goose Publications, 2005.

Iona Abbey Worship Book, Compiled by The Iona Community, Wild Goose Publications, 2001.

Liturgies for the Journey of Life, Dorothy McRae-McMahon, SPCK, 2000.

Making Liturgy: Creating rituals for worship and life, edited by Dorothea McEwan, Pat Pinsent, Ianthe Pratt and Veronica Seddon, Canterbury Press, 2001.

Making the Most of Weddings, Andrew Body, Church House Publishing, 2007.

New Patterns for Worship, The Archbishops' Council, Church House Publishing, 2002.

Out of the Ordinary: Prayers, poems and reflections for every season, Joyce Rupp, Ave Maria Press, 2000.

Pocket Prayers for Marriage, compiled by Andrew and Pippa Body, Church House Publishing, 2004.

Prayer Rhythms: Fourfold patterns for each day, Ray Simpson, Kevin Mayhew, 2003.

Prayers Encircling the World: An international anthology of 300 contemporary prayers, compiled by SPCK, SPCK, 1998.

Prayers for Life's Particular Moments, Dorothy McRae-McMahon, SPCK, 2001.

Present on Earth: Worship resources on the life of Jesus, Wild Goose Worship Group, Wild Goose Resource Group, Wild Goose Publications, 2002.

Seeing Christ in Others, edited by Geoffrey Duncan, Canterbury Press, 2002.

The Enduring Melody, Michael Mayne, Darton, Longman & Todd, 2006.

The Prophet, Kahlil Gibran, Pan Books Ltd, 1991.

The Rhythm of Life: Celtic daily prayer, David Adam, SPCK, 1996.

This Sunrise of Wonder: Letters for the journey, Michael Mayne, Fount, 1995.

Tides and Seasons: Modern prayers in the Celtic tradition, David Adam, SPCK, 1989.

Times and Seasons: Services and prayers for the Church of England, The Archbishops' Council, Church House Publishing, 2006.

Using Common Worship – Marriage, Stephen Lake, Church House Publishing and Praxis, 2000.

Watching for the Kingfisher, Ann Lewin, Inspire, 2004.

Wedding Liturgies, Flor McCarthy, Dominica Publications, 1989.

Words by the Way, Ann Lewin, Inspire, 2005.

Your Marriage in the Church of England, The Archbishops' Council, Church House Publishing, 2003.

A SELECTION OF GRACES FOR THE WEDDING FEAST

Grace
Tessa Wilkinson

As N and N share this meal together as a married couple,
may it be the first of many meals shared with family and friends
May there always be …
a welcome at their door
a space at their table
and a generosity of spirit.
God bless all who sit here today:
May they leave rejoicing in the knowledge of God's love for them.
Amen

Grace
Tessa Wilkinson

As we share food together today, let us thank God
for the farmer who grew it,
for the shop who sold it,
for the chefs who cooked it,
for the people who will serve it.
Grown, harvested, prepared and served by others
so that we can come and celebrate today.
We thank you, God, for this feast
and for all who have played a part in bringing it to this table.
Praise God!
Amen

Grace
Jan Brind

Heavenly Father,
We thank you for this joyful day.
You have filled N and N with your abundant love,
they have made their marriage vows
and now they are man and wife!
You spread a feast before us
and for this we ask your blessing.
In days and years to come
may there always be a welcome in their home,
a place at their table, and food to share.
Amen

Grace
Jan Brind

May God
whose love surrounds us,
whose joy overflows in us,
whose hope sustains us
be present at this wedding feast.
May this food and this wine
be blessed and shared
as we give thanks and praise to God!
Amen

Grace
Tessa Wilkinson

N and N ...
Like the champagne bubbles – may you fizz.
Like the candle's flicker – may you be people of light.
Like the music that plays – may you skip through life.
Like the pillars on the wedding cake – may you stand firm in God's love.
May you be blessed by God today, and through all your days together.
Amen

Grace
Tessa Wilkinson

The bride and the bridegroom have come to the feast:
May God bless them!
Their family and friends are gathered around them:
May God bless them!
We remember those not able to be here:
May God bless them!
May the blessing of God: Father, Son and Holy Spirit
be with us all as we share this feast together.
Amen

Grace
Jan Brind

O God, you send us from above
Your gifts of joy and wondrous love.
As now we gather here to dine,
Please bless to us this food and wine.
Amen

Grace
Tessa Wilkinson

The family is gathered,
The guests have arrived,
The vows are exchanged,
The marriage is blessed,
The tables are laid,
The food is prepared,
Let us break bread together:
Praise God and rejoice!
Amen

Grace
Jan Brind

This is the day the Lord has made!
With love and joy and hope inlaid!
We give him thanks, before we dine,
For broken bread and jugs of wine.
May God the Father, our high priest,
Send down his blessing on this feast!
Amen

HYMNS AND SONGS

Be still and know
    God, whose love is all around us
    May the Lord bless you
    May you walk with Christ beside you
    This world you have made

Celtic Hymn Book
    Deep peace of the running wave
    Father, give your love
    God of life be with you
    Love is patient
    May the peace of the Lord Christ go with you
    Praise to the Lord
    The love of Christ surround us
    This day God gives me
    We swear by peace and love
    Where the love of Christ unites us

Hymns of Glory, Songs of Praise
    Brother, sister, let me serve you
    I come with joy
    Let's praise the Creator who gave us each other
    Like the murmur of a dove's song
    Lord of our growing years
    Put peace into each other's hands
    She sits like a bird, brooding on the waters
    The grace of life is theirs
    Your love, O God, has called us here
    We come, dear Lord, to celebrate
    When the bonds of love are breaking

Common Ground
As two we love are wed
Now go in peace

Go Before Us
Christ beside us
Take my gifts
Word of God

Complete Anglican Hymns Old and New
A new commandment
Be still, for the presence of the Lord
Come on and celebrate
Jesus, stand among us at the meeting of our lives
Let there be love shared among us
Life is great!
Such love

Hymns Old and New – New Anglican Edition
All things bright and beautiful
Dear Lord and Father of mankind
Lead us, heavenly Father, lead us
Lord, for the years
Lord of all hopefulness
Love divine, all loves excelling
Now thank we all our God
O perfect love
The Lord's my shepherd
Through all the changing scenes of life

Hymns Old and New: One Church, One Faith, One Lord
God, in the planning
May the grace of Christ our Saviour
O God, beyond all praising
The love we share
These vows of love are taken
We gather here

Laudate
Hear us now, our God and Father
Jesus, Lord, we pray
Lord of all loving
O Father all creating
Surprised by joy
When love is found

Liturgical Hymns Old and New
Let love be real
Love is patient

Love from Below
God beyond glory
Lord and lover of creation
That human life might richer be

New Start Hymns and Songs
At the heart of all things
Living God, your word has called us
Lord, we thank you for the promise

One is the Body
Love is the touch
Love one another

Songs of Fellowship
Jesus put this song into our hearts
O, heaven is in my heart
You are the vine

Songs of God's People
As man and woman we were made
I will enter his gates
You shall go out with joy

21st Century Folk Hymnal
Wherever you go

*The sheet music for 'Love changes everything' from the musical Aspects of Love
by Andrew Lloyd Webber is available from The Really Useful Company.*

A SELECTION OF HYMN BOOKS AND SONG BOOKS

CDs or cassettes are available for titles marked with an asterisk.

Material published by OCP Publications, GIA Publications, the Taizé Community, or Wild Goose Publications, is available from Decani Music. Wild Goose Publications are also available from the Wild Goose Resource Group Online Shop.

Anglican Hymns Old and New, compiled by Kevin Mayhew, Kevin Mayhew, 2008.

Be Still and Know, compiled by Margaret Rizza, Kevin Mayhew, 2000.

Cantate: A book of short chants, hymns, responses and litanies, edited by Stephen Dean, Decani Music, 2005.

Celebration Hymnal for Everyone, edited by Patrick Geary, McCrimmons, 1994.

Celtic Hymn Book, selected by Ray Simpson, Kevin Mayhew, 2005.

Children's Praise, compiled by Greg Leavers and Phil Burt, Marshall Pickering, 1991.

*Christ, Be Our Light, Bernadette Farrell, OCP Publications, 1994.

Christe Lux Mundi, music from Taizé, Instrumental Edition, Ateliers et Presses de Taizé, GIA Publications, 2007.

*Christe Lux Mundi, music from Taizé, Vocal Edition, Ateliers et Presses de Taizé, GIA Publications, 2007.

Church Hymnary, fourth edition, editorial panel convened by the Church of Scotland and led by John L. Bell and Charles Robertson, Canterbury Press, 2005.

*Come all You People, shorter songs for worship, John L. Bell, Wild Goose Publications, 1994.

*Common Ground, a song book for all the churches, John L. Bell and Editorial Committee, Saint Andrew Press, 1998.

Common Praise, compiled by Hymns Ancient & Modern Ltd, Canterbury Press, 2000.

Complete Anglican Hymns Old and New, compiled by Geoffrey Moore, Susan Sayers, Michael Forster and Kevin Mayhew, Kevin Mayhew, 2000.

*Drawn to the Wonder, hymns and songs from churches worldwide, compiled by Francis Brienen and Maggie Hamilton, Council for World Mission, 1995.

Enemy of Apathy, John L. Bell and Graham Maule, Wild Goose Publications, 1988 (revised 1990).

*Fire of Love, Margaret Rizza, Kevin Mayhew, 1998.

*Fountain of Life, Margaret Rizza, Kevin Mayhew, 1997.

Gather (second edition), edited by Robert J. Batastini, GIA Publications, 1994.

*Gift of God, Marty Haugen, GIA Publications, 2001.

Glory and Praise (second edition), Oregon Catholic Press, 2000.

*Go Before Us, Bernadette Farrell, OCP Publications, 2003.

*God Beyond all Names, Bernadette Farrell, OCP Publications, 1991.

*Heaven Shall Not Wait, John L. Bell and Graham Maule, Wild Goose Publications, 1987 (reprinted 1994).

Hymns and Psalms, British Methodist Conference, Methodist Publishing House, 1987.

Hymns of Glory, Songs of Praise, editorial panel convened by the Church of Scotland and led by John L. Bell and Charles Robertson, Canterbury Press (on behalf of the Church Hymnary Trust), 2008.

Hymns Old and New, New Anglican Edition, compiled by Geoffrey Moore, Susan Sayers, Michael Forster and Kevin Mayhew, Kevin Mayhew, 1996.

Hymns Old and New: One Church, One Faith, One Lord, compiled by Colin Mawby, Kevin Mayhew, Susan Sayers, Ray Simpson and Stuart Thomas, Kevin Mayhew, 2004.

*I Will Not Sing Alone, John L. Bell, Wild Goose Publications, 2004.

Iona Abbey Music Book: songs from the Iona Abbey Worship Book, compiled by The Iona Community, Wild Goose Publications, 2003.

*Light in our Darkness, Margaret Rizza, Kevin Mayhew, 2002.

Laudate, edited by Stephen Dean, Decani Music, 2000.

Liturgical Hymns Old and New, compiled by Robert Kelly, Sister Sheila McGovern SSL, Kevin Mayhew, Father Andrew Moore and Sister Louisa Poole SSL, Kevin Mayhew, 1999.

*Love and Anger: songs of lively faith and social justice, John L. Bell and Graham Maule, Wild Goose Publications, 1997.

*Love from Below, John L. Bell and Graham Maule, Wild Goose Publications, 1989.

*Many and Great: World Church songs Vol. 1, John L. Bell and Graham Maule, Wild Goose Publications, 1990.

Methodist Hymns Old and New, compiled by Revd Peter Bolt, Revd Amos Cresswell, Mrs Tracy Harding and Revd Ray Short, Kevin Mayhew, 2001.

Mission Praise, compiled by Roland Fudge, Peter Horrobin and Greg Leavers, Marshall Pickering, 1983.

New Hymns and Worship Songs, Kevin Mayhew, 2001.

New Start Hymns and Songs, compiled by Kevin Mayhew, Kevin Mayhew, 1999.

**One is the Body: Songs of unity and diversity*, John L. Bell, Wild Goose Publications, 2002.

**Psalms of Patience, Protest and Praise: 23 Psalm settings*, John L. Bell, Wild Goose Publications, 1993.

Rejoice and Sing, Oxford University Press, 1991.

**Restless is the Heart*, Bernadette Farrell, OCP Publications, 2000.

*River of Peace, Margaret Rizza, Kevin Mayhew, 1998.

**Sacred Dance: Celtic music from Lindisfarne*, Keith Duke, Kevin Mayhew, 2005.

**Sacred Pathway: Celtic songs from Lindisfarne*, Keith Duke, Kevin Mayhew, 2004.

**Sacred Weave: Celtic songs from Lindisfarne*, Keith Duke, Kevin Mayhew, 2003.

**Sent By The Lord: World Church songs Vol. 2*, John L. Bell and Graham Maule, Wild Goose Publications, 1991.

*Share the Light, Bernadette Farrell, OCP Publications, 2000.

Sing! New Words for Worship, Rosalind Brown, Jeremy Davies and Ron Green, Sarum College Press, 2004.

Sing Glory: Hymns, psalms and songs for a new century, edited by Michael Baughen, Kevin Mayhew, 1999.

**Songs and Prayers from Taizé*, Ateliers et Presses de Taizé, Continuum, 1991.

Songs and Prayers from Taizé: Cantor and instruments, Ateliers et Presses de Taizé, GIA Publications, 1991.

Songs for Prayer, Ateliers et Presses de Taizé, Ateliers et Presses de Taizé, 1998.

Songs for Prayer: Instrumental, Ateliers et Presses de Taizé, Ateliers et Presses de Taizé, 1998.

Songs of God's People, The Panel on Worship, Church of Scotland, Oxford University Press, 1988 (reprinted 1995).

Songs from Taizé, Ateliers et Presses de Taizé, Ateliers et Presses de Taizé, published annually.

Songs of Fellowship, compiled by members of Kingsway Music Editorial Team, Kingsway Music, 1991.

*Tales of Wonder, Marty Haugen, GIA Publications, 1989.

The Children's Hymnbook, compiled by Kevin Mayhew, Kevin Mayhew, 1997.

The New English Hymnal, compiled by Anthony Caesar, Christopher Dearnley, Martin Draper, Michael Fleming, Arthur Hutchings, Colin Roberts and George Timms, Canterbury Press, 1986 (reprinted 1999).

The Source 3: Definitive worship collection, compiled by Graham Kendrick, Kevin Mayhew, 2005.

*There is One Among Us: Shorter songs for worship, John L. Bell, Wild Goose Publications, 1998.

*Walk with Christ, Stephen Dean, OCP Publications, 1996.

World Praise, David Peacock and Geoff Weaver, Marshall Pickering, 1993.

Worship (third edition), edited by Robert J. Batastini, GIA Publications Inc., 1986.

21st Century Folk Hymnal, compiled by Kevin Mayhew, Kevin Mayhew, 1999

USEFUL CDs

A Bride's Guide to Wedding Music
Naxos

Favourite Wedding Music
21 favourite tracks performed by Malcolm Archer, David Briggs and Noel
Rawsthorne
Kevin Mayhew Ltd

Favourite Wedding Music
Stephen Cleobury
Belart

Music for Civil Weddings 2
Wedding Music

Music for Weddings
Classic FM – Music for Weddings
Classic FM

Music for Your Wedding
Featuring Katherine Jenkins, Kiri te Kanawa and St Paul's Cathedral Choir
Marks & Spencer

NT – The Wedding Album
Two hours of the most romantic wedding music
Sony Bmg

The Complete Wedding Album
Telarc

USEFUL WEBSITES

There is a huge number of wedding sites on the internet. Here are just some of them.

Fireworks

www.hitched.co.uk
Celebration displays of fireworks.

Liturgy

www.cofe.anglican.org
This has the *Common Worship* marriage service online.

Magicians

www.weddingchaos.co.uk

Music

www.weddingguide.co.uk
Selection of hymns and music with online listening.

www.mfiles.co.uk
Live and sheet music.

www.2-in-2-1.co.uk
Hymns

Readings and Poems

www.weddingguide.co.uk
Love poems, readings and quotations.

www.youandyourwedding.co.uk

Transport

www.classic-touring.co.uk
Classic cars for hire.

www.fireenginefun.co.uk
Fire engines for transport (in Sussex).

www.freewheelerautos.com
Tuk Tuks for hire (in Hampshire).

www.weddingchaos.co.uk
Rolls Royces to horse-drawn carriages.

www.travelwithhunny.com
Routemasters and open-topped buses for hire.

Venues

www.ultimatevenue.com
www.topchart.co.uk
Weddings on board sailing barges or tall ships (River Thames).

ACKNOWLEDGEMENTS

Marriage Service – Basic Service

Kahlil Gibran, 'On Marriage', *The Prophet*, Pan Books (an imprint of Macmillan Publishers Ltd.), 1991.

Marriage Service when the Couple are Older

Thomas Hardy, *Far from the Madding Crowd*, Oxford University Press, 2002.

Marriage Service in Church after Divorce

Ann Lewin, *Words by the Way – Ideas and resources for use throughout the Christian year*, Inspire, 2005. Used with the author's permission.

Renewal of Marriage Vows for More than One Couple

Michael Mayne, *This Sunrise of Wonder*, Fount, 1995.

Healing Prayers in Church at the Ending of a Marriage

Eugene H. Peterson, *The Message Remix*, NavPress Publishing Group, 2003.